Victorious Japanese soldiers in the Philippines assemble around a mammoth artillery piece, to pose in triumph for a photograph that will be sent back home.

THE RISING SUN

Other Publications:

THE GREAT CITIES
HOME REPAIR AND IMPROVEMENT
THE WORLD'S WILD PLACES
THE TIME-LIFE LIBRARY OF BOATING
HUMAN BEHAVIOR
THE ART OF SEWING
THE OLD WEST
THE EMERGENCE OF MAN
THE AMERICAN WILDERNESS
THE TIME-LIFE ENCYCLOPEDIA OF GARDENING
LIFE LIBRARY OF PHOTOGRAPHY
THIS FABULOUS CENTURY
FOODS OF THE WORLD
TIME-LIFE LIBRARY OF AMERICA
TIME-LIFE LIBRARY OF ART
GREAT AGES OF MAN
LIFE SCIENCE LIBRARY
THE LIFE HISTORY OF THE UNITED STATES
TIME READING PROGRAM
LIFE NATURE LIBRARY
LIFE WORLD LIBRARY
FAMILY LIBRARY:
   HOW THINGS WORK IN YOUR HOME
   THE TIME-LIFE BOOK OF THE FAMILY CAR
   THE TIME-LIFE FAMILY LEGAL GUIDE
   THE TIME-LIFE BOOK OF FAMILY FINANCE

Alexandria, Virginia

WORLD WAR II · TIME-LIFE BOOKS · ALEXANDRIA, VIRGINIA

BY ARTHUR ZICH
AND THE EDITORS OF TIME-LIFE BOOKS

THE RISING SUN

Time-Life Books Inc.
is a wholly owned subsidiary of
TIME INCORPORATED

Founder: Henry R. Luce 1898-1967

Editor-in-Chief: Hedley Donovan
Chairman of the Board: Andrew Heiskell
President: James R. Shepley
Vice Chairman: Roy E. Larsen
Corporate Editor: Ralph Graves

TIME-LIFE BOOKS INC.

Managing Editor: Jerry Korn
Executive Editor: David Maness
Assistant Managing Editors: Dale Brown,
Martin Mann
Art Director: Tom Suzuki
Chief of Research: David L. Harrison
Director of Photography: Melvin L. Scott
Senior Text Editors: William Frankel,
Diana Hirsh
Assistant Art Director: Arnold C. Holeywell

Chairman: Joan D. Manley
President: John D. McSweeney
Executive Vice Presidents: Carl G. Jaeger (U.S. and
Canada), David J. Walsh (International)
Vice President and Secretary:
Paul R. Stewart
Treasurer and General Manager:
John Steven Maxwell
Business Manager: Peter G. Barnes
Sales Director: John L. Canova
Public Relations Director: Nicholas Benton
Personnel Director: Beatrice T. Dobie
Production Director: Herbert Sorkin ·
Consumer Affairs Director: Carol Flaumenhaft

WORLD WAR II

Editorial Staff for *The Rising Sun:*
Editor: William K. Goolrick
Picture Editors/Designers: Thomas S. Huestis,
Charles Mikolaycak
Text Editors: Thomas H. Flaherty Jr.,
Valerie Moolman, David Thomson
Staff Writers: Ruth Kelton, Henry P. Leifermann,
Philip W. Payne, James Randall,
Sterling Seagrave, L. Robert Tschirky
Researchers: Josephine G. Burke,
Doris Coffin, Jane Edwin, Barbara Fleming,
Gail Nussbaum, Josephine Reidy,
Henry Weincek, Frances G. Youssef
Editorial Assistants: Cecily Gemmell,
Dolores Morrissy

Editorial Production
Production Editor: Douglas B. Graham
Operations Manager: Gennaro C. Esposito
Assistant Production Editor: Feliciano Madrid
Quality Director: Robert L. Young
Assistant Quality Director: James J. Cox
Associate: Serafino J. Cambareri
Copy Staff: Susan B. Galloway (chief),
Margery duMond, Victoria Lee,
Mary Ellen Slate, Florence Keith,
Celia Beattie
Picture Department: Dolores A. Littles,
Barbara S. Simon
Traffic: Barbara Buzan

Correspondents: Elisabeth Kraemer (Bonn); Margot
Hapgood, Dorothy Bacon (London); Susan Jonas,
Lucy T. Voulgaris (New York); Maria Vincenza Aloisi,
Josephine du Brusle (Paris); Ann Natanson (Rome);
Villette Harris (Washington). Valuable assistance was
also provided by: Ralph Iula (Akron); Wibo van de
Linde (Amsterdam); Karen Horton (Honolulu);
Carolyn T. Chubet, Zenona Green (New York);
S. Chang, Shoichi Imai, Frank Iwama (Tokyo).

The Author: ARTHUR ZICH, formerly a staff
member of LIFE. SPORTS ILLUSTRATED. TIME and
Newsweek, is a freelance writer who specialized
in Asian studies at Dartmouth and Yale. While
stationed in Okinawa with the U.S. Air Force, he
served as a Chinese interpreter and later spent
three years covering Southeast Asia from TIME's
bureau in Hong Kong. He lives in Half Moon
Bay, California, and is at work on a book about
the Philippine Islands.

The Consultants: COL. JOHN R. ELTING, USA
(ret.), is a military historian, author of *The Battle
of Bunker's Hill* and *A Military History and Atlas
of the Napoleonic Wars.* He was the editor of
*Military Uniforms in North America: The
Revolutionary Era* and served as associate editor
for *The West Point Atlas of American Wars.*

JOHN M. MAKI is a professor of political science at the University of Massachusetts at
Amherst. A specialist in Japanese government
and politics, Professor Maki is the author of
*Japanese Militarism: Its Cause and Cure;
Government and Politics in Japan: The Road to
Democracy; Court and Constitution in Japan;*
and several other books and numerous articles
dealing with Japan. In 1946, he served as civilian
consultant on reorganization of the Japanese
government at General Headquarters, Supreme
Commander for the Allied Powers in Tokyo.

CHAPTERS

PICTURE ESSAYS

CONTENTS

A DOOMED WAY OF LIFE

Baggy-shorted Britons take up their positions for a brisk go at rugby in front of the Federal Secretariat Building at Kuala Lumpur in the 1923 Malaya Cup final.

THE LAST DAYS OF COLONIAL GLORY

The Prince of Wales and a few friends follow the action at Singapore's polo grounds during the Prince's 1921 tour of Britain's Far Eastern empire.

Most European colonists in Southeast Asia drowsed through the years between the World Wars, secure in their white ducks, their pith helmets and the conviction that their empires were immortal. The British in Burma, Malaya and Borneo ("Out East") and the French in Indochina shared the view propounded by a governor general of the Netherlands East Indies: "We Dutch have been here for three hundred years; we shall remain here for another three hundred."

A transplanted European life style insulated the colonists from the natives, whom they tended to regard as quaint, exasperating subhumans. The British forgathered in clubs that banned nonwhites—and any Caucasians who consorted too openly with Asians. Britons trusted implicitly in "the Raj" (an all-inclusive term for British rule), and they lived for afternoon tea, amateur theatricals, showy official ceremonies, and outdoor sports; in 1935 Singapore alone had 2,000 tennis courts and six golf courses.

Life in the French colonies revolved around a civilized cuisine, the native mistress—often hired by the week—the apéritif, the bidet and a cumbersome bureaucracy that bristled with forms, stamps and seals. Saigon had the best theater in the Orient and the Hanoi opera house could seat the city's entire European population.

The Dutch, less aloof than the British or the French, washed down huge meals with torrents of gin and beer, wore sarongs around home and intermarried freely with natives. But they ruled their 70 million Indonesian subjects rigidly, paid peasants a mere four cents a day and gave no more heed than the French or British to the nationalist movements already undermining all three empires.

The dream life ended abruptly when Japanese armies surged down the Malay Peninsula—while a few Britons in Singapore, unable to comprehend what was happening, continued to dance nightly at the Raffles Hotel. Some never did comprehend. One Englishwoman who survived the terrible debacle later explained it: "The British Raj was one of the most wonderful things in the world, but when the Raj ended everyone started killing each other."

A diminutive native bearer provides a common colonial service—toting a hefty French official along the bed of a jungle stream in the wilds of Indochina.

The splendidly uniformed Dutch Governor Tjarda van Starkenborch-Stachouwer and his white-gowned daughter entertain the Sultan of Solo, his wife and an interpreter in 1940 at the governor's palace in Batavia (now Djakarta). Above them looms a portrait of their exiled Queen Wilhelmina, who had fled to England after Holland fell to the Nazis.

Guests at an Indonesian hotel in the 1920s are feted with the famous 32-dish rice table, served by ranks of waiters, each bearing a different delicacy. Onto a base of rice, successive servitors piled chicken, duck, eggs, sausages, fish, meatballs, fried bananas, potatoes and grated coconut while other waiters heaped side dishes with sauces and relishes.

British notables bestow their blessing on a loyal vassal by attending a war dance at the 1932 installation of a Malay tribal chief. At center rear, Lady Caldecott (dark glasses), wife of the Chief Secretary of the Federated Malay States government, sits between Chief Abdul Rahman Ibni Muhammad and his wife. In a white uniform, to the left of the chief's wife, is Major General Louis Oldfield, then Commander-in-Chief of British forces in Malaya.

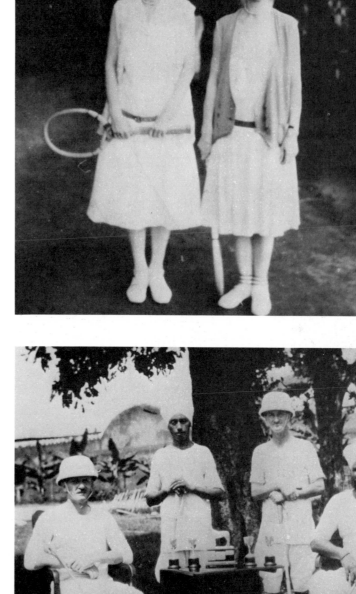

Pictures from a family album portray life on the Burmese frontier. At the mountain outpost of Sinlumkaba (above, left), Vivian Clerk (center) of the frontier service has tea with his wife, Beatrix (holding dog), and Anne Jacob, wife of the local military police chief. On Christmas in 1928, Beatrix and Anne (right, above) played tennis at the nearest club, which was a mud hut in Bhamo, two days' journey away by muleback. At right is a polo team composed of Major Rupert Jacob (left), his second-in-command, Captain Harvey Stubbs, and two of the Indian army officers who were then stationed in Burma.

On a visit to Singapore during a tour of the Far East in 1920, former French Premier Georges Clemenceau (back to camera) sits with the colony's beplumed

governor as members of the local French community and representatives of the diplomatic corps wait for him to dedicate a new avenue named in his honor.

1

On September 6, 1941, behind the tree-lined moat of Tokyo's old Imperial Palace, in Room No. 1 East, a meeting was under way in which Japan would formally adopt a policy that would change the shape and destiny of half the world. On a raised dais before an ancient gold screen, Emperor Hirohito of Japan, Son of Heaven, the 124th in an unbroken line of earthly deities that reached back 2,600 years, sat silent in a crisp military tunic. His narrowed eyes gazed intently through heavy lenses at two brocade-covered tables, behind which the members of the Japanese Cabinet and of the Supreme Command, the nation's highest-ranking civilian and military officers, sat stiff as mannequins, hands upon their knees.

For two hours, these men rose in turn, bowed to the Emperor, and described the desperate situation confronting their nation. The Foreign Minister began by declaring that the United States, Great Britain and the Netherlands were marshaled against the Japanese Empire. The National Planning Board Director warned that the economic blockade these countries had imposed on oil and other raw materials was strangling Japan. The Navy alone was consuming 400 tons of oil every hour. The Navy Chief of Staff stated that the nation's fuel reserves would not last through the coming year. His Army counterpart grimly assented.

After hearing them all, Yoshimichi Hara, the President of the Privy Council and the man who stood between the Cabinet and the Throne, spoke tersely. "Starting now," said Hara, "we will prepare for war."

The Emperor then did an extraordinary thing. Raised to reign but not to rule, and trained to acquiesce in Cabinet decisions, Hirohito drew a small slip of paper from his pocket and in his high nasal voice read a poem that had been written by his grandfather, Emperor Meiji:

All the seas everywhere
  are brothers to each other.
Why then do the winds and waves of strife
  rage so throughout the world?

It was the first time since five years earlier, when he had spoken out against an Army rebellion, that Hirohito had broken the traditional Imperial silence at a council of state; his action stunned the men assembled.

However, it did not change their minds. The decision had

COUNTDOWN FOR WAR

already been made, and adopted by the Army and Navy on September 3, to carry through the fateful program: if, by the first week in November, the diplomats of Japan's Foreign Office could not persuade President Roosevelt to lift his crippling embargo on oil and other raw materials, then Japan would attack the Pacific territories of the United States, Britain and the Netherlands.

It would be a desperate gamble, as even the most warlike Japanese leaders knew. The United States, by Tokyo's own estimate, had 10 times the production capacity of Japan. Thus the U.S. was sure to win a long war. The commander of the Combined Imperial Fleet, Admiral Isoroku Yamamoto, voiced the warning bluntly. "In the first six to twelve months of a war with the United States and Britain, I will run wild and win victory after victory," Yamamoto declared. "After that . . . I have no expectation of success."

Japan's only hope was in a pair of massive and simultaneous surprise assaults, one on the U.S. naval base at Pearl Harbor, the other on the mainland and the offshore islands of Southeast Asia. These attacks had to be executed with such stunning speed that the Japanese could consolidate their new empire before the United States war machine rolled into high gear. Then, behind a barrier of western Pacific bases that would eventually extend in a wide arc from the Kurile Islands in the north down through Wake Island to the Bismarck Archipelago and New Guinea, Japan might wage a war of attrition that would force the United States to sue for peace, and leave Asia in Japanese hands.

Many of the wiser leaders in both nations had striven for years to avoid such a collision, but they had struggled against overwhelming odds. The roots of the conflict lay deep in the anguished decade from which Japan had just emerged, a period the Japanese were later to call *kurai tanima*, the "dark valley." It was a time of economic distress, of plots and abortive coups and assassinations; a time, most significantly, when the Imperial Army gained virtual control of the government and hatched plans of conquest.

As the decade began, Japan, calm on the surface, was inwardly smoldering. Poverty and the tensions it breeds were everywhere. More than half the population consisted of hard-scrabbling peasants and fishermen, who earned less than one fifth of the national income. Some 80 million people were crowded into the tiny Japanese home islands, mountainous areas about the size of the state of Montana; only a sixth of the land was arable. With 2,900 people per square mile of usable farmland, Japan was the most crowded nation in the world, and its population was growing at a rate of almost a million a year. One means of relief for the hopelessly overmanned agricultural community was to create an alternate way of life by accelerating Japan's industrialization. But the tariff barriers raised by many nations in the decade following the First World War, and the worldwide depression of the 1930s, choked the trade on which Japan's industries lived. The obvious alternative, then, was for the Japanese to find more land to live on.

Japan's need for raw materials was as acute as its need for living space and trade. But Asia's riches were in the grip of Western nations. Burma and Malaya, with their deposits of rubber, tin, tungsten and bauxite, belonged to Great Britain; Indochina's rubber plantations were held by France; the East Indies' vast oil reserves were controlled by the Dutch. Many Japanese, knowing their country was the most advanced in the East, began to feel Japan had a right to these riches. Some were convinced Japan had a divine mission to lead Asia into a new era of economic expansion and prosperity, a "Greater East Asia Co-Prosperity Sphere," as Japanese politicians were calling it by 1940.

The Japanese who held the deepest feeling about their nation's crisis, and were most determined to act, were young officers of the Imperial Army. Many of these junior officers were sons of poor farmers (the Japanese Army promoted on merit, not social rank); they knew the people's misery firsthand. Most of them believed that the nation's problems were attributable to corrupt politicians, and indeed over the past decade the government had been rocked by numerous scandals.

The people of Japan tended to agree with the young officers and looked to the Army to save the nation. The Imperial Army enjoyed great prestige. It still basked in the glory of Japan's triumph over Russia in the war of 1904-1905. It was untainted by scandal. Moreover, it was powerful; an imperial ordinance of 1900 kept it virtually independent of civilian control, a state within a state. Despite the nation's economic plight, the armed forces demanded and got huge budgets. But powerful as they were, the armed forces wanted yet more power.

Intense idealism, poverty and a lust for power make a volatile combination; they exploded throughout the decade of the dark valley. The first serious rumblings reverberated in March 1931. A plan was hatched for a mob, armed by the military with some 300 bombs, to blow up the buildings that housed the Diet (Parliament) and the headquarters of the major political parties. The Army intended to step in amid the confusion and proclaim a military dictatorship. At the last minute General Kazushige Ugaki, who would probably have been installed as a dictatorial prime minister, thought better of the coup and called it off.

But it was a warning of things to come. Only six months later the so-called Kwantung Army, which since 1905 had been guarding Japanese business interests at points scattered through the 440,000-square-mile northern Chinese province of Manchuria, simply seized control. The world was shocked—and more significantly, so was official Tokyo. The Kwantung Army officers had seized Manchuria without any orders whatsoever from the government, and proceeded to rule it as an Army satrapy. Belatedly ordered to stop, the officers ignored the directive. Whereupon, after a considerable amount of sputtering, the government recognized the Army's *fait accompli*, dubbed the acquired territory "Manchukuo" (meaning "State of Manchu") and encouraged people to emigrate there.

The Kwantung Army's surprising and successful adventure on the Asian continent did not quiet the unrest at home. On the contrary, it led to a series of assassinations, as young officers and other superpatriots set out to kill the politicians who had resisted the Manchurian adventure. On February 9, 1932, former Finance Minister Junnosuke Inouye was gunned down on a Tokyo sidewalk. On May 15, nine Army and Navy officers, having prayed to the sun goddess, burst into the home of the 75-year-old incumbent Prime Minister Tsuyoshi Inukai, an opponent of the Manchurian takeover. Inukai, appearing wholly unafraid, politely led them to an inner room where, Japanese style, they removed their shoes. One impatient conspirator, however, became excited and yelled out, "No use talking! Fire!" All nine emptied their guns into the courageous old man.

During the sensational trials that followed these killings, public sympathy flowed not toward the victims, but toward their murderers. The killers had struck a heroic blow for the people against the corrupt politicians. Who else but the military could end the depression? One of Inukai's assassins said the Prime Minister had been "sacrificed on the altar of national reformation." So strong was the outpouring of public sympathy that a group of nine men offered to take the assassins' place in the dock and, to prove their sincerity, accompanied the offer with their nine little fingers, severed and preserved in alcohol. The killers received relatively light sentences; none was condemned to death.

These killings were only a prelude to the bloody Army uprising of February 26, 1936, which because of the date was called the "2-26 Incident." A cabal of young Army officers marched some 1,500 troops out of their barracks at 4 o'clock on that cold, snowy morning and laid siege to the governmental center of Tokyo.

Officers roamed the city, trying to assassinate Admiral Keisuke Okada, who was the new Prime Minister, and much of the Cabinet. The Prime Minister escaped by hiding under dirty laundry in a closet when the killers came to his house. Not so fortunate was Finance Minister Korekiyo Takahashi, loathed because he had resisted the previous year's large military budget. After rampaging through his house, breaking down doors, the killer-officers found Takahashi in his bedroom. A lieutenant kicked the quilt off the Minister and yelled *"Tenchu!"* meaning "Punishment of Heaven." Takahashi yelled back "Idiot!" before he was shot and killed. Another officer slashed at Takahashi, severing an arm, then stabbed him in the stomach. At this point Takahashi's distraught wife appeared. The young lieutenant bowed and said, "Excuse me for the annoyance I have caused."

Another victim was a former prime minister, Viscount Makoto Saito, a moderate, intellectual, gentle man. Saito and his wife had spent the evening before as dinner guests of the United States Ambassador to Japan, Joseph C. Grew. After dinner there had been a screening of the sentimental American musical *Naughty Marietta*, with Jeanette MacDonald and Nelson Eddy. It was an appropriate film to show the Saitos, Grew felt, because it had, in his words, "no vulgarity whatever." The Saitos left the embassy at 11:30, a late hour for them. By dawn the next morning Saito was dead, his body pierced by 36 bullets.

After four days of killings, the terror ended as abruptly as

AUDACIOUS GRAB FOR AN EMPIRE ON THE PACIFIC

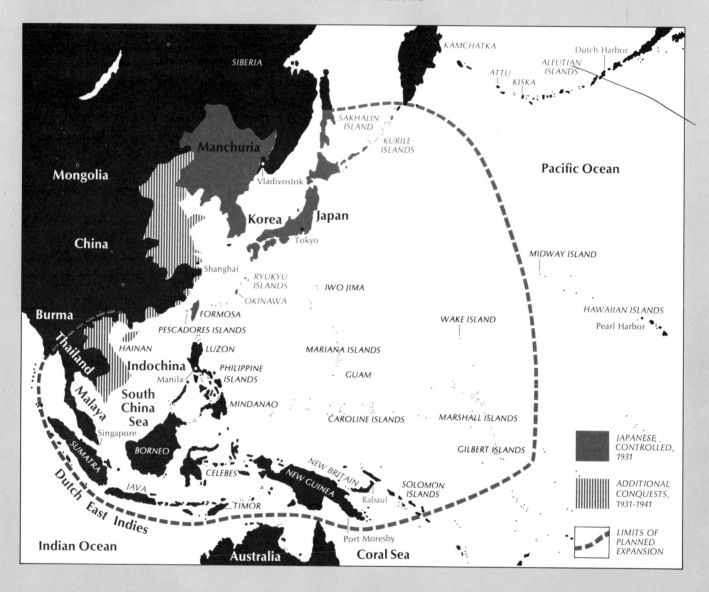

In September 1941, the rulers of Japan decided upon a desperate gamble—they would seize control of the riches of Asia by expanding their empire to the limits indicated by the dashed line on the map above.

The Japanese had already outgrown their home islands. Between the turn of the century and 1931 they had acquired all of the territory shown above in solid red; they had snatched Manchuria, Korea, Formosa and the Ryukyu and the Pescadores islands from China and had taken southern Sakhalin and the Kuriles away from Russia. The Allies after World War I had also awarded Japan the Marshall, Caroline and Mariana islands, which were formerly held by Germany.

Starting in 1937, Japan extended its sway to the shaded areas on the map, seizing northern China and the main Chinese seaports from Shanghai south to Hainan Island. In July 1941, the Japanese occupied Indochina with barely a nod to the impotent Vichy French officials there. Japan then planned to smash outward, crippling the United States Pacific Fleet at Pearl Harbor and subsequently conquering the Philippine Islands, the Dutch East Indies, Borneo, Thailand, Burma, Malaya, the Solomon Islands, the Gilbert Islands and the isolated American outposts of Guam and Wake Island.

Within six months Japan achieved most of these objectives. Then an ill-considered reach for Midway Island and the Aleutians encountered resurgent Allied resistance that checked—and finally reversed—the tidal wave of Japanese conquest.

it had begun, the insurgent troops returning to barracks on the Emperor's orders. But this time the ringleaders did not get off lightly. Hirohito and many of the senior military officers were becoming alarmed at the killing of high government men. And within the Army, the killers' rivals saw a chance to do away with their competitors; a number were speedily court-martialed and executed.

But the dreadful 2-26 Incident did not discredit the military in the eyes of the people or reduce the Army's political power. Quite the opposite. From February 1936 to the outbreak of war in 1941, Japanese politicians who blocked any of the Army's plans lived in fear of assassination. Further, the Army and Navy chiefs had long enjoyed the prerogative of choosing each Cabinet's War and Naval Ministers. Thus, when the military services' top officers disliked what a Cabinet was doing, they could recall the War and Naval Ministers, and force the Cabinet to fall. In short, the military could virtually dictate any Cabinet's policy.

American Ambassador Joseph Grew watched all this with growing apprehension. Grew was a tall and dignified man, with gray hair and startlingly black and luxuriant eyebrows. Like the proper Bostonian he was, he had gone to Groton preparatory school and Harvard College. At both institutions he had known Franklin D. Roosevelt, who was two classes behind Grew. The Ambassador was a passionate golfer. When actor Douglas Fairbanks visited Japan, he and Grew played 36 holes in one day—in the rain. Grew delighted the Japanese, who were enthusiastic about both golf and baseball, by playing a round of golf with visiting baseball heroes Babe Ruth and Lefty O'Doul.

Grew was also a serious, experienced and adept diplomat. He understood Japan remarkably well, thanks in large measure to his wife, who had grown up in Japan and knew the language perfectly. "Whatever way it falls out," Grew wrote in his diary, "one thing is certain and that is that the military are distinctly running the Government and that no step can be taken without their approval."

Grew had been named ambassador in 1932. By 1934 he was warning Washington that Japan had designs on all of East Asia. "When Japanese speak of Japan's being the 'stabilizing factor' and the 'guardian of peace' of East Asia, what they have in mind is a *Pax Japonica*," he advised. The next step, he said, would be "complete political control."

"There is a swashbuckling temper in the country," Grew concluded, that might lead the government to "any extremes" and eventually to "national suicide."

Not even the perceptive Grew, however, foresaw what was to happen next. On July 7, 1937, a detachment of patrolling Japanese troops met a Chinese unit near Peking, at an ancient bridge named after Marco Polo. A skirmish ensued and a few soldiers fell. This was sufficient excuse for Major General Kenji Doihara to lead the Kwantung Army, which already had slid into parts of northern China to protect Japanese businesses there, to launch a major attack.

Before long what the Japanese called the "China Incident" developed into a full-scale war. More troops and

TOJO   IIDA   HOMMA   IMAMURA   YAMASHITA

Few soldiers ever entered upon a war with less enthusiasm than General Hideki Tojo, Japan's Prime Minister and Minister of War. His misgivings about taking on the Western Allies were shared by the four lieutenant generals entrusted with Japan's conquest of Southeast Asia: Shojiro Iida in Burma, Masaharu Homma in the Philippines, Hitoshi Imamura in the Dutch East Indies, and Tomoyuki Yamashita in Malaya. All of these middle-aged, combat-hardened veterans had served abroad and all respected their opponents' potential strength. But once ordered into battle, the four field commanders proved themselves to be among the world's ablest generals, and in six months they overran more territory than any conqueror since Napoleon.

ships were rushed to reinforce Doihara's forces. With them came Japanese Army and Navy planes, modern bombers to smash defenseless Chinese cities. One after another, the cities—Peking, Tientsin, Shanghai—fell to the Japanese. The poorly equipped Chinese, under 51-year-old Generalissimo Chiang Kai-shek, fell back after each major engagement, losing hundreds of thousands of lives.

Chiang's withdrawal kept his battered army reasonably intact. But it also left a large part of the nation naked in the face of an increasingly ruthless foe. In the Kiangsu Province of eastern China, the Japanese marched into the virtually defenseless city of Nanking and reduced it in sadistic fashion. Some 20,000 Chinese men of military age were marched out of the city and used for bayonet practice, machine-gunned or doused with gasoline and set on fire. Perhaps 20,000 women and girls were raped, killed or mutilated. Thousands of other civilians were murdered and robbed. As many as 40,000 Chinese were slaughtered before what came to be called the "Rape of Nanking" was over.

It seems clear the Japanese officers, who talked of bringing a Japanese-inspired "renaissance" to Asia, had intended the massacre to terrify the Chinese into making peace. The plan failed. Chiang spurned negotiation with Tokyo; in October 1938 he retreated farther into China's vast interior, moving the capital from Hankow to Chungking. Assisted by a Communist guerrilla leader named Mao Tse-tung—with whom he had a temporary alliance of convenience—Chiang shored up his defenses and refused to quit.

The Japanese tried to pursue him and lay siege. But the enormous expanse of China, served by only a threading of dirt roads, seemed to swallow up the million or more advancing Japanese troops. China became a quagmire for the Imperial Army. And the more deeply Japan became involved in China, the more sharply the Tokyo government found itself in collision with the West, especially with the United States, which at the time nurtured a sentimental fondness for China. In October 1937, President Roosevelt gave a speech condemning Japan's aggression. A leading Japanese, Yosuke Matsuoka, soon to be Foreign Minister, lashed back: "Japan is expanding and what country in its expansion era has ever failed to be trying to its neighbors? Ask the American Indian or the Mexican how excruciatingly trying the young United States used to be."

American concern was increasing, but the President's ability to respond was restricted. Americans were overwhelmingly isolationist. Even when Japanese planes intentionally bombed the American gunboat, the *Panay*, in the Yangtze River on December 12, 1937, there was no inclination to fight. When news of the incident reached Washington, Senator Henrik Shipstead of Minnesota blamed the Americans. "What are they doing there anyway?" he asked. "Why don't they all get out?"

Nevertheless the United States seemed to be awakening to the danger. In January 1938, a month after the *Panay* went down, President Roosevelt asked for and got a 20-per-cent increase in naval appropriations, for the beginnings of a two-ocean navy. At the same time, Roosevelt began to tighten the economic screws on Japan. He called on U.S. manufacturers of munitions and aircraft not to sell those items to Japan so long as they were used for the slaughter of Chinese. The arms boycott was strictly voluntary—a "moral embargo"—but it worked.

A year and a half later, in October 1939, the President quietly took his first military step toward Japan: he ordered the U.S. Pacific Fleet from its traditional home base of San Diego to the mid-Pacific. Henceforth it would operate from Pearl Harbor on the Hawaiian island of Oahu. Roosevelt knew the Navy was not ready for major offensive operations, and the defenses at Pearl Harbor were weak. Still, he felt the westward move of a mass of capital ships would be a clear message to Japan.

The Japanese were far from deterred. Indeed, their impulse toward further expansion was encouraged by Hitler's 1940 blitzkrieg in Europe. As the German armies rolled over the Netherlands and France and then gathered themselves for an invasion of Britain, the Dutch, French and British colonies in Asia suddenly seemed ripe for plucking. On August 1, 1940, Ambassador Grew warned that Japanese militarists now saw "a 'golden opportunity' to pursue their expansionist desires unhampered by the allegedly hamstrung democracies." And Grew added, "The German military machine and system and their brilliant successes have gone to the Japanese head like strong wine."

A new Cabinet had just taken over in Japan. It was headed by Prince Fumimaro Konoye, a hesitant, quiet man who was overshadowed by two other Cabinet members: the strong-willed Minister of War, Lieut. General Hideki Tojo; and the Foreign Minister, Yosuke Matsuoka. Arrogant, ambitious, and dazzlingly brilliant—some thought him mad—Matsuoka had been raised and educated in Portland, Oregon, and he fancied himself an expert on America. "It is my America and my American people that really exist," Matsuoka once declared grandly. "There is no other."

His colleagues conceded him that expertise, and gave him a freer hand in conducting Japanese foreign policy than any previous Foreign Minister had had. Matsuoka's main problem was that he could not keep his mouth shut. One moment he would send U.S. Secretary of State Cordell Hull a message overflowing with expressions of good will; the next, he would tell an American newspaper correspondent that democracy was finished, that the fascist states would inevitably win the war and there was no room in the world for two systems of government. Hull quite naturally decided the Japanese government in general, and Matsuoka in particular, could not be trusted. Hull's suspicion of Japan's motives would become a factor in bringing on war.

This mounting distrust was deepened, ironically enough, by an important United States triumph: American cryptographers had cracked Japan's highest diplomatic code. From August 1940 on, they could intercept the secret cable traffic between Tokyo and Japan's overseas embassies. The intercepts were given the code name Magic. So whenever Hull listened to the latest diplomatic peace offers from Japan's ambassador to Washington—a hearty, sincere, guileless ex-admiral named Kichisaburo Nomura—he would have already read Magic intercepts indicating that Japan was not really bent on peace, but rather was preparing for war. Hull was a stiff-backed mountain man from Tennessee with an ingrained loathing for duplicity and double-dealing. His straight-on Protestant mind believed that diplomacy could and should be carried on in a forthright, honest, open fashion. Slow to anger, he was capable of deep hatred when aroused. And he was coming to hate the Japanese.

On September 27, 1940, Foreign Minister Matsuoka made a major move that did nothing to reassure Hull. He signed a pact firmly aligning Japan with Germany and Italy. Almost immediately Japan put pressure on the Dutch to sell more of their East Indian oil. At about the same time, the Japanese pressured the French shadow government in Vichy to allow Japanese troops to be stationed in French Indochina—later to be called Vietnam. Japan's announced reason was that it needed troops in Indochina to cover the southern flank of the China campaign. But to Hull—and to Roosevelt and Churchill—it plainly looked as if Japan was getting itself in position to invade Burma or Malaya, possibly to attack the great British base at Singapore. The French gave in, and Japanese soldiers and aircraft poured into Indochina.

Roosevelt and Hull had known for some time that the move was coming. Magic intercepts, including one containing the entire ultimatum to Vichy, had tipped them off. In July 1941, while Japanese troops were going ashore at Cam Ranh Bay and occupying Saigon and Da Nang in Indochina, Roosevelt announced a complete embargo of all oil shipments to Japan. He had already reduced petroleum and cotton consignments to the Japanese, and had embargoed shipment of other vital materials, such as scrap iron, as one way of trying to warn Japan to abandon the war in China. Now all Japanese assets in America were frozen and all United States trade with Japan was cut off. Britain and the Netherlands followed suit.

The Japanese were deeply disturbed by these measures. A flurry of conferences followed, involving top Japanese military and political leaders. Emissaries were sent to Washington to help the plodding Nomura. But the Japanese position and that of the United States remained desperately far apart. Hull and Roosevelt indicated that the oil tap would not be turned on again unless Japan got out of Indochina, and China as well—and also renounced the Tripartite Pact with Germany and Italy. The Japanese replied that the notion of getting out of China was unthinkable; they had invested too many men and too many millions of yen in the China Incident to pull out now. On the contrary, they wanted the United States to get out of China—that is, to stop sending arms to Chiang.

Despite the tremendous gap between the two nations' basic positions, the diplomats struggled, especially the seemingly tireless Grew. He wrote long letters to his old schoolmate pleading for greater understanding of Japanese psychology. The Japanese should not be made to conclude that they were cornered, Grew wrote the President, for they would

Twelve years before Pearl Harbor, Admiral Kichisaburo Nomura (front left), his staff and the Japanese consul general (in formal civilian attire) join U.S. Major General Edwin Winans (center) and staff at Fort Shafter in Honolulu for a picture-taking session. The 1929 visit by Nomura—to be ambassador to the United States on December 7, 1941—was one of the annual calls on U.S. Pacific bases made by Japan's top naval officers in the prewar years. On these seemingly innocuous visits the emissaries gauged U.S. strength and reinforced ties with overseas Japanese.

feel impelled to lash out. By now the impetuous Matsuoka had been replaced as Foreign Minister by the level-headed Admiral Teijiro Toyoda. On the hottest evening of August 1941, Grew talked for hours with Toyoda—"the longest conversation," Grew said, "that I have ever had with any Foreign Minister." As Grew wrote down Toyoda's remarks, "It was drip, drip, drip, so after the first hour Admiral Toyoda ordered cold drinks and cold wet towels to swab off with. He made a gesture to take off his coat and looked at me smilingly and questioningly. Of course I nodded, so we both took off our coats, rolled up our sleeves, and again pitched in to the work."

In September Grew wrote his boss, Secretary of State Hull, a long, painstaking and closely reasoned cable pleading for what he called "constructive conciliation" rather than "economic strangulation." The Japanese would never agree to abandon their invasion of China, he said; therefore if the United States wanted to negotiate a peace agreement, that demand would have to be soft-pedaled. He heartily endorsed a suggestion made by Toyoda that President Roosevelt meet with the Japanese Prime Minister, Prince Fumimaro Konoye, perhaps in Hawaii. He warned Secretary Hull that the Japanese were entirely capable of entertaining two contradictory ideas at once—that they could prepare for war and at the same time sincerely search for peace.

Hull would not be persuaded. Although Roosevelt was more than willing to meet Prime Minister Konoye, the Secretary of State torpedoed the idea. Hull had in his desk a fateful *Magic* intercept that revealed Japan's plans to take over both Indochina and Thailand; thus, he simply did not believe that the Japanese had any intention of giving up their plans for the conquest of Asia.

Both Hull and FDR were under great pressure to be unbending toward Japan. Washington was full of noisy pro-Chinese partisans who kept public opinion whipped to a froth. The leader of the "China Lobby" was T. V. Soong, a brother-in-law of Chiang Kai-shek. Chiang himself bombarded Hull and Roosevelt with what Hull called "hysterical" cables, urging that the United States send him more supplies and money, and arguing against any compromise with the Japanese.

There was some pressure, too, from FDR's Cabinet. The Secretaries of Navy and War, Frank Knox and Henry L. Stimson, counseled taking a strong line, since they were convinced that Japan either was bluffing and would prove unwilling to fight, or was too weak militarily to do much

damage if it did go to war. This position was echoed inside Hull's State Department by the head of the Asia desk, Stanley Hornbeck. He, too, believed Japan was bluffing and he thought that the United States could easily defeat any Japanese military moves within six months.

There was pressure to be firm from Churchill as well. He even drafted strong notes that he urged Roosevelt to sign and send to Tokyo. Roosevelt did not send the notes, nor did he allow his friend Churchill to dictate United States policy. FDR, to the last, wanted to reach some accommodation with Japan. The possibility that the United States might become directly involved in the struggle against Hitler was never far from his mind and he knew that one war at a time was more than enough. Indeed, General George Marshall, Chief of Staff of the Army, and Admiral Harold R. Stark, Chief of Naval Operations, had told him the U.S. armed forces were far from ready to fight *any* war.

The various pressures on Roosevelt and his Secretary of State increased through the autumn of 1941. Grew kept warning from Tokyo that war could come with dangerous and dramatic suddenness. Two last attempts were made to avoid a conflict. The Japanese envoys in Washington presented a short-term plan, a kind of *modus vivendi,* that did not solve all the fundamental issues but at least offered some bargaining points. In exchange for resumption of oil shipments from the United States, Japan would cease military moves in Southeast Asia and, once peace with China was restored or an overall peace in the Pacific established, would withdraw troops from all foreign soil. Hull called the plan "preposterous."

Roosevelt, fearing an end to negotiations, had penciled in his own *modus vivendi*—a resumption of economic relations with Japan in return for an end to Japanese troop movements north and south and a renewal of peace negotiations with China. This plan, too, might have provided a basis for further diplomatic talks, but the Japanese never saw it. As Hull was pondering FDR's proposal, on the night of November 25, word came from U.S. Army Intelligence that a huge Japanese convoy of warships and troop transports was steaming through the China Sea toward Southeast Asia and perhaps the Dutch East Indies. What was the use of presenting a conciliatory proposal to a nation so evidently bent on war? Roosevelt's plan was laid aside.

Instead, Hull sent off to Tokyo a document later to be known as his Ten Points—10 stern conditions reaffirming the fundamental demand that Japan turn the clock back to 1931 by getting out of Indochina, China and Manchuria, and by renouncing their Tripartite Pact with Germany and Italy. Why Roosevelt let Hull substitute this outright challenge for his own moderate approach is not clear. The Secretary's sense of moral outrage seems at this point to have overborne his boss's reservations. Most experts today agree that Hull's diplomacy lacked imagination and flexibility, the very qualities that Grew, who had no illusions about Japan's willingness or ability to wage war, had been urging on his superiors. As Grew could have predicted, the Ten Points struck the Japanese leaders in much the same way as the news of Japanese troop movements had affected Hull. This new evidence of United States intransigence convinced them there was no hope in further negotiation; they must strike now or sit quietly and be strangled.

Throughout that fateful fall, Japan had been perfecting its war plans. The 25th Army, under Lieut. General Tomoyuki Yamashita, was to slice southward down the slender, 600-mile-long Malay Peninsula and take the fortress of Singapore, with its key naval base. The 14th Army, under Lieut. General Masaharu Homma, was to invade the American-owned Philippines—a potential thorn in the eastern flank of Japan's push south. The Japanese Navy and the 16th Army, under Lieut. General Hitoshi Imamura, would seize the biggest prize of all: the oil-rich Dutch East Indies. The 15th Army, under Lieut. General Shojiro Iida, was to step off from Thailand into Burma and close the Burma Road, the last Allied overland supply route from India to China.

The man responsible for the Japanese Navy's war plan was solid and respected, but his attack plan provoked a storm of controversy. No one in Japan was more opposed to war with the United States than Admiral of the Combined Fleet, Isoroku Yamamoto. Yamamoto knew American strength firsthand: he had studied briefly at Harvard and had spent two years in Washington as a naval attaché. "Japan cannot beat America," he told a group of Japanese school children in 1940. "Therefore, Japan should not fight America." Yamamoto had played no part in the decision for war; indeed, he had been sent to sea to get him out of range of would-be assassins who thought his antiwar views unpatriotic. But now that the decision for war was made, Yamamoto was adamant on one point: it was imperative that Japan destroy the U.S. Fleet at Pearl Harbor.

Every member of the Navy General Staff opposed the scheme. And the arguments against it were compelling. Surprise was essential for its success—but how could an armada of six aircraft carriers and perhaps two dozen support ships load up, leave Japanese waters and steam halfway across the Pacific undetected? The only route that would avoid commercial shipping was across the chill North Pacific. But how could they refuel under way in these storm-tossed winter seas? If the plan had to be aborted, the Fleet would have been uselessly diverted from the main operation—and might have to fight the United States Fleet in wholly unfamiliar waters. Most important, the inherent risks outweighed the potential gains: there was no *need*, the dissidents argued, to attack the U.S. Fleet.

Yamamoto insisted. Security could and would be maintained; the technical problems could be solved. And as for the need for the attack, he asserted: "The U.S. Fleet . . . is a dagger pointed at our throat. Should war be declared . . . the length and breadth of our southern operations would be exposed to serious threat on its flank." But only when Yamamoto threatened to resign his commission and retire if the plan was not approved, did the General Staff concede. "If he has that much confidence," declared the Navy Chief of Staff, "it is better to let Yamamoto go ahead."

He was already well along in preparations. At Kagoshima, a small southern city topographically similar to Honolulu, hand-picked squadrons of Japanese Navy pilots had been practicing pinpoint bombing and torpedo attacks since late summer. So incessant was the din of aircraft engines that the hens in one seaside village quit laying eggs. At night, the flyers pored over a model of Oahu seven feet square and studied silhouettes of the U.S. ships at Pearl Harbor until they could call out their names at a glance. Meanwhile the Japanese Consul General in Honolulu had been cabling back weekly coded reports on U.S. Fleet movements, harbor berthing positions and duty schedules. The Fleet, Yamamoto noted, was in port every Saturday and Sunday. The Army's proposal for a strike on Sunday, December 8, Tokyo time (December 7, Washington time) would be fine.

By late November, Yamamoto had imposed radio silence on *Kido Butai* (the Pearl Harbor Strike Fleet), and ordered other Japanese warships on the Inland Sea to send out a flurry of bogus messages. He charted a course that would take the force down a lonely slot between Dutch Harbor in the Aleutians and Midway Island, just beyond range of U.S. air patrols. For staging, he chose a remote harbor in Japan's frozen Kurile Islands called Hitokappu Bay.

At 6 a.m. on November 26, the Strike Fleet weighed anchor and, under strict radio silence, slid out into the chill North Pacific waters. A patrol boat at the harbor mouth flashed a message: "Good luck on your mission." The dark gray flagship carrier *Akagi* signaled "Thanks." At the flight deck control post beneath *Akagi*'s bridge, Captain Mitsuo Fuchida, the commander of the Pearl Harbor Air Strike Force, looked back as the Kuriles' rugged mountains, like a Hiroshige landscape painting, receded into the mists. Down on deck *Akagi*'s crew also took a last look at their homeland and roared a lusty "*Banzai!*" Fuchida was profoundly moved. "I realized my duty as a warrior," he wrote later. "I thought at the time, 'Who could be luckier than I?'"

Twelve days later, just before dawn on December 7 (Hawaiian time), the Japanese Strike Force reached the launch point, 230 miles due north of Oahu, just as other Japanese forces around the rim of Asia were nearing their destinations. In the central Pacific the sky was still dark, the horizon not yet visible. The big ships heaved ponderously in heavy seas, kicking foamy white spume off black waters and hurling plumes of stinging sea spray over carrier decks. Ground crews clung desperately to the fighters and bombers now lined up wing to wing.

Well before dawn the engines started turning over, hurling propwash back with the wind; wing lights trembled as the planes strained at their moorings. Yamamoto's final message had clicked in over the wireless, echoing the rallying cry of the commander of the victorious Japanese Fleet at the Battle of Tsushima against Russia 36 years before: "The rise or fall of our Empire now hinges on this battle." From the flight deck the green light flashed for takeoff. From the cockpit of the lead fighter, Captain Fuchida yelled to his crew chief: "Kick out the blocks!" The plane lurched forward, gathered speed and lifted itself into the still-dark sky. In a matter of moments, the sun would rise.

GEARING FOR BATTLE

Gargantuan sound detectors of preradar days, aimed skyward like huge ear trumpets, dwarf Emperor Hirohito (left, front) as he inspects Tokyo's defenses.

TOTAL MOBILIZATION, EMPEROR TO CHORINE

A bemedalled Hirohito seated on a white charger parades with officers of the Imperial Army during a 1937 New Year's Day military review in Tokyo.

Through the 1930s Japan's war-hawk leaders channeled the nation's resources toward conquest with ever-increasing intensity. Soldiers led factory workers in daily compulsory calisthenics and lectured them on civic virtue. Public contributions supplemented already-bloated military budgets; school children gave small change to build a battleship, and geishas pooled their tips to buy a warplane. Japanese athletes at the 1936 Olympic Games in Berlin wore army caps; nightclubs put on military shows for which the chorines *(right)* were taught correct small-arms techniques.

The greatest privilege for the common man in Japan was the universal two-year tour of military service, and the highest honor was death in combat. The men were inducted into and mustered out of the services with elaborate ceremonies. While in uniform they gladly endured one of the world's most rigorous army regimens. A Japanese infantryman trained 14 hours a day, six days a week and might march 25 miles a day for weeks on end, laden with gear weighing two thirds as much as he did. Exceptionally hot or cold weather brought extra drill for special toughening. Holidays were celebrated by adding a sham battle or other vigorous exercise to the normal schedule. Long hikes were finished at a run to prove to the men they still had reserves of strength. Troops stayed busy night and day during maneuvers. "They already know how to sleep," said one officer. "They need training in how to stay awake."

But though the soldiers were tough, their equipment was meager. Even after Japan's industry regeared for modern production in the late 1930s, the horses in an infantry division outnumbered motor vehicles 10 to 1. Light machine guns were few, electronic equipment primitive, and the infantryman's basic weapon was a clumsy bolt-action rifle. Still, all weapons, new or old, were lovingly cared for. Soldiers treated rifles with almost the same reverence that officers lavished on samurai swords; and though few were crack shots, most were artists with the bayonet. Above all, soldiers and civilians alike were imbued with the idea that to survive, Japan must fight—and win.

Preparing for a militaristic stage routine, dancers of an Osaka nightclub are supervised by an Army officer to assure a soldierly bearing, even in pantomime.

A delegation parades through Tokyo in 1938 with bugles blaring and flags flying to escort a Japanese draftee to his new home—an army barracks. Inductions were always ceremonial occasions. A form letter sent to each recruit's father and elder brother promised that the Army "will be to him a stern father and a loving mother." All dressed up and accompanied by his family, the rookie then reported for duty, mindful that any lapse might bring the unbearable shame of a note from his commanding officer telling his parents he was failing in his duty to the Emperor.

In a tree-lined exercise ground, Japanese troops wielding padded poles line up for bayonet drill, a vigorous daily ritual for enlisted men. Officers engaged in equally strenuous bouts of fencing with two-handed swords.

Tokyo's Mayor Tomejiro Okubo (second from left) and several other municipal officials participate in rifle marksmanship practice at the Toyama Military Academy in 1940.

Soldiers of the Imperial Bodyguard demonstrate wall-scaling skills during 1935 maneuvers in Tokyo, pitting the Bodyguard against the Army's First Division.

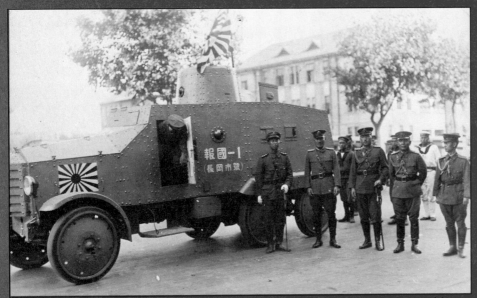

Imperial Marines guard one of the relatively few armored vehicles in Japan's prewar armed forces.

Tractor-drawn artillery, here parading past ranks of troops, was another rarity in the pre-1940 Army.

A mobile smithshop, used to shoe Army horses, includes a built-in forge and portable lights.

Kimono-clad geishas gather around a reconnaissance plane purchased by the Shimbashi Guild of Tokyo Geishas for the Japanese Army in 1933. Between 1937 and December 1941, Japan's Army and Navy air strength grew from a total of 1,378 planes to nearly triple that figure.

Crack Imperial Marines march proudly behind a Rising Sun standard-bearer at Yokosuka Naval Station on January 19, 1937, to celebrate Japan's termination of the Washington Conference treaty that had limited the size of the Japanese Navy. Freed of all restraints, Japan quickly built a fleet powerful enough to challenge the might of United States and British forces in the Pacific.

GOOD DUTY IN THE ISLANDS

Sailors on liberty at Honolulu's Waikiki Beach take snapshots of shipmates and a young Hawaiian woman perched aboard an outrigger canoe.

BEFORE THE BOMBS BEGAN TO FALL

Until about 1940 the war spreading across Europe and Asia barely touched the lives of U.S. servicemen, even in the nation's most far-flung outposts, the bases scattered across the vast Pacific. The chief concerns of the men stuck on sun-scorched coral islets like Wake and Midway were to dodge work details and gun drills, and to avoid dying—of boredom. A few eager officers fretted about shoring up defenses, and spoke darkly of the Japanese threat. But the waking hours of more typical servicemen were spent trying to wangle a transfer from their own lonely rocks to those twin paradises of the Pacific—Hawaii and the Philippines.

In Hawaii, there were sparkling beaches as well as soothing breezes, and women, too—lots of them, and friendly. And though enlisted men felt welcome in some first-class Honolulu hotels only when in civvies, there were plenty of other places to have fun. For example, a man could sample the barroom battles in dives like the Black Cat near the Honolulu servicemen's YMCA—although some complained that Hawaiian men could be too handy with broken bottles.

The Philippines had their special lures. There, for a few cents a day, a soldier could hire a native "bunk boy" to make his bed, shine his shoes, wash his clothes and even pull KP in his stead. On most days his time was his own after 2 p.m. and 10-day passes were easily come by. And many a trooper swore that Philippine girls were the prettiest in the Pacific. One seaman on shore leave in Manila even managed an affair with Josephine Oswald, a Filipina film star.

By 1941 there was a bustle of new construction throughout the Pacific islands, an influx of planes, ships and men, a series of alerts and maneuvers, a hint of trouble in the air. Even so, Major General Lewis H. Brereton later recalled that when he reached Manila on November 3, 1941, to take command of the Far East Air Force, he found work and training schedules were "still based on the good old days of peace conditions in the tropics." On weekends there and in Hawaii, ships and bases were manned only by skeleton crews. "The idea of imminent war," said Brereton, "seemed far removed from the minds of most."

U.S. warships lying at anchor in Manila Bay frame a diver at the Army and Navy Club pool just a week before the Japanese attack on the Philippines.

Undisturbed by a passing flight of U.S. Army Air Forces B-17 and A-20 bombers, bathers splash in the warm waters of Waikiki Beach, in Honolulu, Hawaii.

During maneuvers off Hawaii, cooks aboard the battleship Idaho line up for coffeepot inspection—one of the many navy rituals aimed mostly at keeping all hands busy.

Sailors belly up to the Idaho's soda fountain for the low-priced refreshments listed on the sign behind the mess boy's head. Such amenities were standard on large ships and at most shore bases—where servicemen could buy everything from milk shakes to cameras.

PRICE LIST
SOFT DRINKS 5¢
COFFEE 5¢
SINKERS 5¢
ICE CREAM, PTS. 10¢
GE-DUNKS 10¢
CHOC MILK 5¢
COOKIES 5¢
SANDWICHES 10¢
MALTS 10¢
SHAKES 10¢
SODAS 10¢
BARS 5¢

Beneath a satiric poster of shore leave, two young officers in the wardroom of the cruiser Indianapolis match tactics in chess.

With his crew braced against the gun's concussion, an officer gives the signal to fire a mortar during a drill on the Philippine fortress of Corregidor.

Members of a Corregidor gun crew on stand-by alert chat and clean weapons in one of the island's bombproof and gasproof tunnels.

Artillerymen in an underground magazine on Corregidor use a chain hoist to raise shells to the guns that are emplaced on the surface.

A week before the Japanese attack on the Philippines, Navy men enjoy an evening in an ornate Manila dance hall.

At Manila's posh Polo Club, football fans munch an early breakfast while listening to a short-wave broadcast of the Stanford-California football game.

2

Mitsuo Fuchida flung back his cockpit canopy and surveyed the awesome air fleet he commanded. He could not see all the planes, but enough were in sight to reassure him everything was ready. Directly aft, strung out through billowing towers of white clouds, were the leaders of the 48 blunt-nosed, single-engine Nakajima-97 bombers like his own, each carrying a 1,760-pound armor-piercing bomb. To his right and slightly below, Fuchida could see some 40 more torpedo bombers, whose projectiles were designed for shallow harbor water. To the left and a little above were 51 stubby Aichi dive bombers. And high overhead, their dual machine guns and twin 20mm cannons at the ready, droned 43 Mitsubishi Type-O fighters—the fast, deadly "Zeroes" soon to dominate Asia's skies. On each plane's fuselage and wingtips blazed the neat red disk of the Rising Sun—as much a religious symbol as a national insignia.

Ahead, beneath a thick cloud blanket, lay Fuchida's target, Pearl Harbor. This was to be the most daring strike in the massive surprise attack Japan had already launched across the breadth of the western Pacific. Even as Fuchida's planes neared Hawaii, a Japanese task force was shelling the dark, forested coast of Malaya; other troops were assaulting British pillbox positions on Kota Bharu's shores and swarming over Thailand's beaches at Singora and Pattani, clearing the way for a coordinated drive down the 600-mile-long Malay Peninsula to the British bastion of Singapore. Meanwhile Japan's air arm would soon begin bombing the Philippines, Guam, Wake Island and the British Crown Colony of Hong Kong. The key move in this far-flung and deadly chess game was the destruction of the U.S. Pacific Fleet, lying at anchor at Pearl Harbor. And this move depended on the skill of the 39-year-old commander of the air armada winging south above the bright Pacific.

The time was 0700. Fuchida switched on his radio. Hawaiian music filtered faintly through his headphones. He twisted his antenna until the music was loudest; then, bearing on it, he made a 5° course correction. Fuchida twisted the dial again; over the wind and engine roar he heard what he was hoping for. "Partly cloudy," the Honolulu announcer stated. "Clouds mostly over the mountains. Visibility good. Wind north at ten knots." Fuchida rejoiced. "What a windfall for us!" he exclaimed.

The planes came in over Kahuku Point, Oahu's northern

THE SURPRISE ATTACK

tip, banked to the right and flew down the island's west coast: the torpedo bombers wanted to make their final run from the south, low over the water. As the planes approached the target area, Pearl Harbor was clearly visible to Fuchida. Peering through binoculars, he scanned the blue water closely, and a stunning spectacle came into view. He carefully counted the ships below, lying quietly at anchor. "They're all there, all right," he thought exultantly.

Seven towering gray vessels were lined up on "Battleship Row," on the eastern edge of Ford Island, in the center of the harbor. That would be the *California,* at the southwestern end of the row; then, moored together in pairs, the *Maryland* and the *Oklahoma,* the *Tennessee* and the *West Virginia,* the *Arizona* and the repair ship *Vestal,* and finally, alone at the northeastern end of the row, the *Nevada.* An eighth battlewagon, the flagship *Pennsylvania,* lay in dry dock with the destroyers *Cassin* and *Downes,* at the Navy Yard across the channel from Battleship Row. Nine cruisers, another 29 destroyers and an array of lesser ships were ranged around the harbor at bollards or moorings. In all, 94 vessels were densely clustered in an area not three miles square, with but one channel to the open sea and a single torpedo net stretched across the channel's mouth. "Never, even in the deepest peace," Fuchida later recalled, had he seen a target so thoroughly unprotected.

He glanced at his watch. It was 0749. He ordered his radioman: "Notify all planes to launch attacks." The signal went out plain: "*To-, to-, to-,*" first syllable of the word *to-tsugeki*—"Charge!" Then, looking down at the U.S. Fleet lying at his mercy, he flashed to his fleet and to Tokyo a fateful message: "*Tora, tora, tora*"—"Tiger, tiger, tiger"—signifying that the attack was a complete surprise.

Beneath Fuchida's attacking force, Pearl Harbor stirred lazily in the Sunday morning sun. At 7:50 a.m. much of the civilian population was still asleep. Sunrise had been at 6:26, but the rain-filled clouds over Mount Tantalus and Mount Olympus on the south side of the island had obscured the sun until nearly 7 o'clock. The light northern breeze made the palm fronds rattle. There were few other sounds—a distant automobile horn along the twisting Nuuanu Valley road, the squawk of a pet parrot, the echo of surf on Diamond Head. In the warming sunlight, rich with the smell of frangipani, patios were still empty, their umbrellas folded. Oahu lay in helpless torpor.

It was not as if there had been no warnings. As America's negotiations with Japan had neared impasse, Washington had sent numerous advisories to its Pacific outposts—the Philippines, Guam, Wake, Hawaii, even the Panama Canal Zone. The U.S. Army Signal Corps had broken the *Purple* code, Japan's cipher for top-priority diplomatic communications, and had been decoding secret Japanese messages for over a year. These messages clearly indicated that Japan was preparing for war.

There were other sources of information about Japanese plans, as well. Japanese secret agents on the island of Oahu had been advising Tokyo by phone of U.S. military dispositions. A United States law forbade the tapping of telephones, including those of alien Japanese, but the Office of Naval Intelligence and the FBI often ignored the law and listened in on these calls. One of them, overheard shortly before December 7, had revealed that the Japanese were burning the files at their Honolulu consulate.

The Navy reported that the Japanese had changed their communications call signals twice within the past month. Normally such changes were made every six months or so; such an abrupt switch was unprecedented. What should have been more ominous news was the Navy's report that it had picked up no radio signals at all from the aircraft carriers of Japan's First and Second fleets, and therefore had not known their locations, since November 16. When Admiral Husband E. Kimmel, Commander-in-Chief of the Pacific Fleet, was told by his intelligence officer on December 2 that the carriers were still unaccounted for, he was appalled. "Do you mean to say," he barked, "they could be rounding Diamond Head and you wouldn't know it?"

Admiral Kimmel had reason for his frosty rejoinder. Everyone knew Japan was going onto a war footing. Everyone expected to hear of a Japanese attack on nearly any country in the Far East (though certainly not on Hawaii, halfway across the Pacific). On November 27 Admiral H. R. Stark, Chief of Naval Operations, had sent an urgent message from Washington to the Pacific admirals. It read: "This dispatch is to be considered a war warning. . . . An aggressive move by Japan is expected within the next few days." But, he added, the evidence "indicates an amphibious expedition against either the Philippines, Thai or Kra Peninsula or possibly Borneo." There was no mention of Hawaii.

Despite all the indications of trouble brewing, no one was upset. Everything could be explained. Intelligence officers reasoned the Japanese carriers were out of radio contact because they were in home waters. Japanese call signals could have been changed because of preparations for a massive fleet movement south from Japan, where most evidence indicated the Japanese were about to move. The phone calls from Oahu to Japan were not disturbing: Japanese on the Islands had been telephoning home to friends and relatives for years. And the report of paper-burning? The Americans, too, burned secret papers periodically.

Besides, warnings of every sort—reports of Japanese destroying their codes, false submarine sightings, tales of spying throughout the islands—had poured into Pearl Harbor's intelligence offices for months. They were nothing new.

What the intelligence officers did not know was that these warnings were different. On a tapped telephone line, the FBI had heard a cook in the Japanese consulate excitedly tell a friend in Honolulu that consular officials were burning *all* important documents. This was a crucial piece of information: the Japanese were not just burning surplus documents, they were destroying everything. Moreover, the FBI knew the burnings were being conducted secretly in the consulate, not outdoors where they might be observed.

The FBI agents had reported none of this critical detail; to have done so would have disclosed their illegal telephone taps. They reported only what they felt was important—and the Navy intelligence officers did not press them for more. They merely assumed these latest reports were more of the same—the significance of the information was lost.

Adding to the general sense of false security in Hawaii was an illusion of American invincibility. The Japanese, the Americans told themselves, would not dare attack Pearl Harbor, or risk the wrath of the mighty U.S. Navy. If anybody *had* experienced a doubt he would have kept it to himself—or at least within his own service. There was an almost complete lack of cooperation among the American military forces in Hawaii; members of the various branches were friendly but made little effort to work together or share information. The climate and comfort of Hawaii also helped lull American forces. No one hurried to get things

done or to work a full day in the langorous, tropical setting.

On Sunday morning, December 7, there were two last-minute warnings that might have saved the day, but both were discounted by the people who might have acted.

At 3:42 on the morning of December 7, the watch officer of the U.S. minesweeper *Condor* sighted something suspicious as the *Condor* was making a pass across the entrance to Pearl Harbor. It looked like the periscope of a submerged submarine. By blinker light the *Condor* signaled the destroyer *Ward*, patrolling nearby. The *Ward*'s skipper, Lieutenant William Outerbridge, was awakened by his gunnery officer. In his Japanese kimono, Outerbridge came on deck and stared out across the dark sea. It was the first patrol of his first command, and he took no chances. He ordered a call to general quarters. All hands on deck searched the waters, while the *Ward* crisscrossed a wide pattern for half an hour. No periscope could be seen. Nothing registered on the sound-detection gear. Outerbridge sent the crew back to their bunks, while those on regular watch maintained the lookout. No message was sent to headquarters; there had been so many false sightings Outerbridge did not want to look foolish by reporting another.

Three hours later, at 6:40, the *Ward*'s helmsman spotted another periscope. Lieutenant Outerbridge came on deck again. This time there was no mistake: a small conning

The first U.S. newspaper to announce the Pearl Harbor attack was the Honolulu Star-Bulletin, published only seven miles from the scene of the action. The paper normally did not appear on Sundays, but editor Riley Allen was in his office when the attack started. He called in reporters and printers and got out four extras before the day was over.

tower was clearly visible only 100 yards from the *Ward*. It was headed toward the harbor. Outerbridge ordered an attack. The *Ward* opened fire. No. 1 gun missed, but No. 3 gun scored a bull's-eye on the conning tower. The sub began to sink, as the *Ward*'s crew cheered. Outerbridge ordered four depth charges and radioed headquarters: "We have attacked, fired upon and dropped depth charges upon submarine operating in defensive sea area." It was 6:53 a.m.

The headquarters message center, at this hour on Sunday morning, was manned by Lieut. Commander Harold Kaminski and a telephone operator. Kaminski, a reserve officer who had been in and out of the Navy since World War I, was the one U.S. military man that morning who actually concluded from the evidence that the war was on. His orders were, in case of attack, to call Admiral Kimmel's chief of staff and the aide to Rear Admiral C. C. Bloch, Commandant of the 14th Naval District. After receiving Outerbridge's message Kaminski tried to call Bloch's aide, but could not reach him. Then he called the Fleet duty officer and Kimmel's chief of staff, Captain John B. Earle. Earle told Kaminski to confirm the *Ward*'s message and to alert the various military departments at Honolulu. Kaminski requested confirmation from the *Ward*, and then started calling the Coast Guard, the War Plans officer and all department heads. The confirmation never came; he was still making calls when the attack began at 7:55.

Meanwhile, Captain Earle called Admiral Bloch to tell him of the *Ward*'s message. The two men concluded that the sub sighting probably was false and that if it was not, the *Ward* and a relief destroyer nearby could handle the situation. They decided to await further developments.

The midget submarine that was sunk had come from the Japanese Advance Expeditionary Force of 27 submarines, five carrying midget subs, all intended to distract U.S. attention from the air attack and cause what damage they could. The force achieved nothing and, through the engagement with the *Ward*, almost gave away the Japanese attack.

The second warning signal was even clearer. The island of Oahu had an Army Aircraft Warning Service consisting of five mobile radar units and an information center at Fort Shafter, just east of Pearl Harbor.

The radar sets had been installed only in recent weeks,

and few operators had mastered them. Nor were the units manned all the time; during December the hours were supposed to be 4 a.m. to 7 a.m. Previously the units had been manned from 6 a.m. to 11:30 a.m., plus a few hours in the afternoon, but in November General Walter Short had changed the times after a war warning from Washington. He considered early morning the most likely hours for an attack. Some of the units operated until 11 a.m.—mostly for training—except on Sundays, when they quit at seven.

One of these portable radar units was set up at Opana, on the northern tip of Oahu. On the morning of December 7, it was manned by two privates, George Elliott, who was new to radar, and Joseph Lockard, who was teaching Elliott how to operate the set and work the plotting board.

There was little to plot. They picked up a suspicious blip at 6:45 and reported it to Fort Shafter, where the operator thanked them and noted it down. Actually it was a Japanese cruiser floatplane reconnoitering ahead of Fuchida's attack force. At 7 a.m. the radar set was due to be shut down. But Elliott wanted to keep it on and practice longer.

At 7:02 he was surprised to see a large blip on the oscilloscope. Lockard, leaning over Elliott's shoulder explaining how the set operated, took over the controls. There on the screen was the largest blip he had ever seen. He checked the set to make sure it was not malfunctioning; it was not. The blip looked like two waves of planes. Working at the plotting board, Elliott placed the planes at 137 miles north, 3° east.

Though new to radar, Elliott understood the blip's significance. He suggested calling the information center; Lockard said that wasn't necessary. Elliott persisted; Lockard said, "Well, go ahead if you like." Elliott tried to reach the information center on his headphone. The line was dead.

He switched to the administration line, an Army telephone, and got through.

"There's a huge number of planes," he reported, "coming in from the north, 3° east."

Private Joseph McDonald, at the information center switchboard, replied that he would record the sighting. But nobody else was there, and McDonald said that he didn't know what he could do about it.

"Well, get someone who does know and let him take care of it," said Elliott. He hung up.

McDonald recorded the report, turned to note the time, and saw an officer at the plotting board in the next room.

Lieutenant Kermit Tyler was an Air Corps pilot assigned to the Aircraft Warning System to learn how radar functioned. McDonald told him about the call from Opana. Tyler was skeptical. He knew of at least two possible flights in the area. The carriers were at sea; on returning to harbor, they usually sent their planes ahead to the Navy airfields. Moreover, a flight of B-17s was due in from the mainland.

But McDonald was uneasy. He called Opana back. Lockard answered. By now he was excited. The screen seemed full of planes, all headed directly for Oahu. McDonald reported that the lieutenant said it wasn't important. Lockard insisted on talking to the officer.

Tyler came to the phone. Lockard argued he had never seen so many planes on his screen. They were now only 92 miles away, and they were coming in at almost 180 mph.

Tyler listened. Then, in one of the more memorable phrases of World War II, he said: "Well, don't worry about it." Then he hung up.

Disgusted, Lockard decided to close down the set. But Elliott wanted to continue watching. The two men studied the screen and clocked the planes' approach: 47 miles by 7:30, 22 miles by 7:39. Suddenly the onrushing wave split in two, as if to come down both coasts of the island. Then there was nothing. The planes had disappeared behind the mountains where the radar pulses could not reach them.

A pickup truck arrived at Opana to take Elliott and Lockard to breakfast. They closed down the station, climbed aboard the truck and headed back to the base camp at Kawaiola. It was 7:50. On their way down, they passed another truck, which was headed back to Opana. It was filled with men in battle helmets. Elliott and Lockard were puzzled, but only until they reached the base camp, nine miles away from the radar installation. The Pacific war had begun. In the confusion that followed the news of the attack on Pearl Harbor, Lockard and Elliott never did get their breakfast.

Aboard the battleship *Oklahoma,* moored to her bollards alongside the battleship *Maryland* in Battleship Row, the forenoon watch had just been piped to breakfast. The men about to be relieved of their watch were wiping the dew off the antiaircraft guns, although only a few of the guns were manned and the ammunition for them was locked up below decks. Other sailors were taking the jack and ensign from the lockers; on the bridge they were readying the Blue Peter signal flag, which was hoisted as a preliminary to raising the Stars and Stripes, when the boatswain piped "To the Colors" at 7:55.

The men about to go on watch enjoyed their last few minutes lounging about the ship. Some were finishing an after-breakfast pipe or cigarette. Across the harbor they could hear church bells for 8 o'clock mass. When the first wave of planes swooped across the bay, nearly everyone thought it was just stunting Navy pilots acting up again.

The Navy and Army commanders in Hawaii, Admiral Husband E. Kimmel (center, at left) and Lieut. General Walter C. Short (above), were relieved from active duty shortly after the attack by the Japanese on Pearl Harbor. Both were held accountable by an investigating committee for not consulting with each other and for failing to put Pearl Harbor on a war footing before the raid.

Suddenly the quiet harbor was bedlam. Explosions erupted aboard half a dozen ships at once. Horns were blaring everywhere. Throughout the *Oklahoma* everyone jumped as the loudspeakers crackled and shouted:

"AIR RAID! NO DRILL!"

The first torpedoes hit the *Oklahoma* with a crump and a boom, and the battleship shuddered like a wounded beast. One sailor later remembered hearing a phonograph playing the popular song, "Let Me Off Uptown." The impact of the first torpedo sent the phonograph into maximum volume, and for a few moments the song blared like a loudspeaker before it abruptly stopped. The next torpedo struck almost immediately after the first. The *Oklahoma's* lights went out; the emergency lights flickered on, went out and came on again. Then the big ship started to list. Within 20 minutes of the first attack, she began to roll over. To one sailor she looked "as if she were tired and wanted to rest." Her bottom rose from the oily water. She kept rolling until her superstructure hit the mud about 25 feet underneath. Then she stopped, looking for all the world like an enormous, beached whale—except for her starboard propeller jutting out of the water.

As the *Oklahoma* rolled to port, the men on deck scrambled to starboard and walked over onto her side, until they found themselves standing upright on her glistening hull. One man then walked along the ship's hull to the bow, waved to a passing boat and jumped in; his shoes were still dry. Some sailors plunged into the water and swam for shore. Others went hand-over-hand along her lines, and were doused when the lines snapped. Still others stood dumfounded on the hull of their overturned battleship and watched the mayhem all around them.

The lead planes of the first wave of attacking Japanese had come in from the southeast, skimming over Merry's Point. As they crossed the harbor, at a distance of 40 to 100 feet above the water, they loosed their torpedoes, which had been specially fitted with new wooden fins in order to prevent them from going too deep. The fins did their deadly work well. The oxygen-powered torpedoes shot through the water just beneath the surface, and streaked straight for their targets.

Forward of the overturned *Oklahoma,* the *California* was punctured by two torpedoes. Oil spewed from her sides like blood. But her guns opened fire, and kept firing throughout the raid, as the *California* settled into the mud.

Aft of the *Oklahoma,* the *West Virginia* began to sink with her decks afire, her guns also keeping up the barrage. One of the garbage lighters swung alongside to help fight her fires. Finally the flames were put out by the harbor waters, but she too sank into the mud; her men, like an army of ants, swarmed into the oil slicks around her.

The *Nevada,* the northeasternmost of those in Battleship Row, was struck in the bow by a torpedo, but her skipper closed off the forward compartments and ordered the ship under way. As the battlewagon moved into the harbor, the dive bombers swarmed over her like hornets. The *Nevada's* guns opened a withering antiaircraft fire, so furious that the big ship almost disappeared in the smoke of her guns. Two Japanese planes were shot down. Fires raged across the *Nevada's* foredeck; one bomb blasted through a starboard gun battery; another detonated a terrific blast below decks, spewing sheets of flame into the air. Still the ship came on, bow down and bleeding oil, smoke billowing behind, but fighting fiercely, clear of Battleship Row now, with the Stars and Stripes fluttering stiffly from her fantail. It was a race for life—a stirring sight even to the attackers.

But if the *Nevada* went down in the channel—and it looked as if she might—her hulk would bottle up the entire Fleet. Accordingly, signal flags went up on the Naval District water tower: stay clear of the channel. Obediently, the *Nevada's* quartermaster nosed the big ship toward shore; two tugs raced to help, and she ran aground at Waipio Point, just short of the channel. The current swung her stern around and left her dead in the water. A half dozen more bombs crashed home on her foredeck and superstructure, but her crew managed to douse her fires and save the ship.

The men remaining on the overturned hull of the *Oklahoma* were surrounded by holocaust. Torpedo bombers and dive bombers screamed down on them, climbed and wheeled to attack them again. Zero fighters strafed them. Bombers soared over them and sent down tumbling sticks of explosives—with deadly accuracy. The morning sky was polka-dotted with antiaircraft fire and stitched with tracers from the attackers and the attacked. Amid the deafening din, roiling clouds of smoke swept across the harbor, and the stench of burning oil was suffocating.

Then came the most thunderous explosion, as the battleship *Arizona* blew up. She had already taken several torpedoes when a bomb scored a hit beside her second turret. It smashed through the deck and exploded in a forward magazine. In one huge convulsion, the bomb and the *Arizona's* ammunition went up. The big battlewagon seemed almost to lurch out of the water. The concussion was felt for hundreds of yards around her. Fiery debris poured over the ships nearby. In an instant the *Arizona* became a towering flame, 500 feet high. Three more bombs found the blazing battleship. Booming and crackling, she sank so fast she had no time to turn over. More than 1,000 men, almost four fifths of her crew, went down in the hissing inferno.

At Schofield Barracks, north of Pearl Harbor, most soldiers had just settled at the mess tables for their Sunday pancakes and extra half-pint of milk when they heard explosions in the distance. "They doing some blasting?" one asked through a mouthful. A plane roared low over the mess hall, its guns firing. Carrying their precious half-pints of milk, the soldiers ran out to see what was going on. Private James Jones (who would someday write a bestseller about Pearl Harbor, *From Here to Eternity*) was standing against the wall when he saw another plane, "with red suns on its wings," which "came up the boulevard, preceded by two lines of holes that kept popping up 80 yards in front on the asphalt." The plane came so close that Jones could clearly see the pilot. A white silk scarf streamed from the pilot's neck, and a *hachimaki,* a white headband, was wound about his helmet, with a red spot at the forehead. As the plane swooped past, the pilot grinned and waved.

At Schofield Barracks—and at many other installations—soldiers and airmen ran for machine guns, mounted them on railings, benches, any support that was available, and fired on the attackers.

The men breakfasting at Hickam Field did not even have time to run out to watch. One of the first dive bombers hit the mess hall. In the shower of crockery, knives, forks and food, 35 men died and many others were wounded, one by a flying gallon jar of mayonnaise. Nearby an Army chaplain had a few moments of warning because he was getting ready for an outdoor mass. Setting up his altar in the open, he saw the planes as they came for the field. He rushed to a nearby machine gun, lugged it over, mounted it on his altar, and sent up an arcing barrage as the planes swooped over him. (His derring-do was later immortalized in a popular song, "Praise the Lord and Pass the Ammunition.")

But at Hickam and at Wheeler Field, 12 miles away, by the time any defense was organized it was too late. Since the November war warning from Washington, precautions had been taken against sabotage, not against air attack. On both fields, the bombers and fighter planes were lined up wingtip to wingtip, so they could more easily be surrounded by guards. The tidy lines of planes were not only sitting ducks, but ducks in rows, and they were systematically destroyed by the Japanese, who had targeted them for the first waves of the attack.

At the height of the first onslaught, the expected B-17s came in after a long flight from the U.S. mainland. They arrived only five minutes after the first bombs fell, and they flew in just east of the track taken by the Japanese.

There were 12 of them. They had flown for 14 hours, and their fuel tanks were nearly dry. To make the distance, the B-17s had been stripped of armor and ammunition and their guns were packed in Cosmoline. The pilots had no warning, and when the first Japanese planes went for them, they thought they were being escorted to their landing field. They were shortly disabused of the notion by flying bullets and by the laconic voice from Hickam's control tower, which provided landing instructions and calmly announced that the field was under attack.

One B-17 was destroyed as it rolled to a halt, its crew jumping out to dash for the nearest cover. Others veered away, with fuel gauges on empty, and pancaked onto small airstrips. One landed on a golf course. Most of the B-17s were damaged, but all but one got through the hail of fire—including some from the Americans below.

While the torpedo bombers and dive bombers were making their runs, Fuchida watched the waterspouts mushrooming up around the ships from a vantage point east of Oahu at 10,000 feet. Then he banked his bomber sharply, the signal for his 10 high-level squadrons to form in single columns for their runs. At that point, Fuchida turned the command over to the squadron's specially trained pilot and bombardier—"the best in the Japanese Navy," Fuchida later recalled. The new commander's plane surged into the van. As it passed,

Fuchida noted the bombardier's round smiling face, and saw him snap off a smart salute.

From Fuchida's orbiting platform, the scene below was an inferno of exploding ships and planes, blazing oil slicks and billowing black smoke. Battleship Row already lay devastated. Only the *Maryland* and the *Nevada,* trapped inboard of the two sinking ships, were comparatively unhurt—and Fuchida's bombers were zeroing in on them.

The American defenders were firing back now. Fuchida was astonished at the speed of their response. "Were it the Japanese Fleet, the reaction would not have been so quick," he recalled. "Dark grey bursts blossomed here and there until the sky was clouded with shattering near misses that made our plane tremble." In the barrage, a Zero exploded in mid-air; a torpedo plane pinwheeled into the water; another, in flames, flew flat out into a United States ship and exploded. Fuchida's wingman was hit; his bombload fell away prematurely and the bomb cinch lines fluttered out like entrails from a gaping wound. The pilot held up a blackboard bearing the message, "Fuel tank destroyed," then asked for and got permission to finish the bomb run. "I knew it was futile," Fuchida said later, "but I understood the feelings of the pilot and crew."

Then Fuchida's own plane bounced "as if struck by a huge club." "The fuselage is holed to port!" his radio operator shouted. "A steering control wire is wrecked." But the plane kept flying. Ignoring the shells bursting around him, Fuchida pulled the safety bolt from his bomb-release lever, and watched the plane ahead; when its bomb dropped, that was Fuchida's signal to drop his bomb. He remembered later that "it seemed as if time was standing still."

Broken clouds scudded by, obscuring the target. The bombardier signaled another run; the planes banked into their turn. "I studied the antiaircraft fire, knowing that we would have to run through it again," Fuchida later wrote. "It seemed that this might well be a date with eternity."

Just then a colossal explosion erupted on Battleship Row. It was the *Arizona.* The shock wave from the blast tossed Fuchida's plane, more than half a mile distant, like a cork on the water. Fuchida's awe-struck pilot shouted, "Terrible!"

Now it was the turn of Fuchida's squadron to run the antiaircraft fire. Their principal target was the *Maryland,* just in front of the furiously smoldering *Tennessee.* The lead plane flashed the "Ready" signal and Fuchida gripped the bomb release again—this time he squeezed it. As the bombs fell, Fuchida watched through a peephole in the floor of his plane. "Four bombs in perfect pattern plummeted like devils of doom," he recounted. "They grew smaller and smaller . . . I forgot everything in the thrill of watching them. . . . They became small as poppy seeds, and finally disappeared as tiny white flashes of smoke appeared on and near the ship." He cried aloud: "Two hits!"

Resuming command, Fuchida ordered his planes back to their carriers as soon as their runs were done. But the commander himself still had work to do. At precisely 0854 —a full 59 minutes after the first bombs exploded—a second wave of raiders swept in around Diamond Head. Fifty-four were bombers, targeting on Hickam and the Naval Air Station at Kaneohe; 81 dive bombers continued the assault on the Fleet; 36 Zeroes backed them up with cannon and machine-gun fire. The dive bombers abandoned their assigned targets—the smoke was too thick to find them—and turned to the ships still hurling up a curtain of fire.

Then, as suddenly as they had come, the attackers vanished. Fuchida made a final pass to photograph the stricken harbor and to attempt, through the thick pall of smoke, to assess the damage before racing back to his carrier, which even then was beginning its run back to Japan's home waters. Fuchida knew the raid had been successful, but he did not entirely grasp the full extent of the destruction that his raiders had left behind.

In a little more than an hour and 45 minutes, the Japanese had destroyed 188 planes and damaged 159 others, and had sunk or seriously damaged 18 ships of war, including the *Arizona* and the *Oklahoma.* The *California, West Virginia* and *Tennessee* would not rejoin the Fleet for months; the *Pennsylvania* and the *Maryland* would be out of action for weeks. In all, the United States had lost 2,403 killed (almost half of them trapped inside the sunken *Arizona*) and 1,178 wounded. On their part, the Japanese had lost 29 planes and pilots, all five midget submarines and one big sub, with their crews. Back on his ship, when he had time to digest the reports, the contented vice admiral in charge of the strike's carrier fleet, Chuichi Nagumo, made his report to his staff. "We may conclude," he said, "that the results we anticipated have been achieved."

TARGET: PEARL HARBOR

On the flight deck of a Japanese carrier, crewmen prepare to release Zero-type fighters revving up for takeoff in the early morning of December 7, 1941.

A DARING TRY FOR A KNOCKOUT BLOW

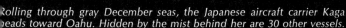

Rolling through gray December seas, the Japanese aircraft carrier Kaga heads toward Oahu. Hidden by the mist behind her are 30 other vessels.

The carrier *Akagi* wallowed in the choppy predawn seas north of Oahu. With her sister ships *Kaga (left), Shokaku, Zuikaku, Hiryu* and *Soryu* and 25 support vessels, she had plowed across the cold North Pacific under orders from Admiral Isoroku Yamamoto to be at this precise spot at 0600 hours on December 7, 1941. On her bridge, Rear Admiral Ryunosuke Kusaka glanced at the lowering sky. He had agreed with Yamamoto that the undertaking was a gamble; now he was acutely aware that even though the ceiling was dangerously low, the winds high, the sea too rough for a safe launch, it was too late to turn back.

As chief of staff of the armada, Kusaka had been one of a few top officers at the center of the meticulous planning begun the year before on a war-game board at the Imperial Naval College in Tokyo. In that mock war the attackers had lost two carriers, but the price was deemed acceptable, and the plans moved ahead. Pilots practiced special bombing and shallow-water torpedo techniques; each flyer received an aerial map of Pearl Harbor photocopied from a postcard bought in Honolulu by a Japanese agent.

Security was kept drum-tight: when the fleet finally got under way on November 26, 1941, most of the crewmen still did not know their destination. Finally, on December 2, the word came down: Pearl Harbor. "An air attack on Hawaii!" thought seaman Iki Kuramoti aboard the *Akagi*. "A dream come true!"

Now, as the time for takeoff approached, crewmen were moving about the misty flight deck, some gathering in quiet knots to pray at portable Shinto shrines. Pilots tied on white *hachimaki* headbands, symbols of their willingness to die for their Emperor. One by one, engines revved; then fighters, torpedo planes and bombers darted off into the sky. Deckbound crewmen sent up a great *"Banzai!"*—a cheer soon to be echoed throughout Japan.

As the planes vanished in the overcast, Kusaka found himself trembling. Ashamed of this loss of control, he sat down to meditate while the force he had launched soared southward toward Pearl Harbor's Battleship Row.

In a frame from captured Japanese propaganda film, carrier pilots purportedly en route to Pearl Harbor listen to radio broadcasts from unsuspecting Honolulu.

A Japanese airman's photograph of Pearl Harbor shows the positions of U.S. battleships and the havoc of the first minutes of the assault. The battleship Nevada, in the left foreground, is still undamaged; beyond it is the Arizona. Farther along, a torpedo trail leads to the West Virginia, hit and bleeding oil, and the Tennessee. Past these lie the Oklahoma, also hit and spilling oil, and alongside it the Maryland. At far right is a seventh battleship, the California. Smoke rises from the cruiser Helena, docked at center, and fires blaze at Hickam Field in the distance.

In Tokyo's Imperial General Headquarters, high-ranking Navy officers, government officials and reporters listen intently as a naval spokesman announces that Japan has "entered into a state of war" with America.

TWO HOURS OF HELL ON A SUNNY SUNDAY

As the first bomb exploded, Gun Captain Jesse Pond and his buddies on the old four-stack destroyer *Chew* wondered how an Army plane could be so careless. "He let his bomb go!" exclaimed one sailor, sure that some stunting U.S. pilot had committed a terrible gaffe. But more detonations followed and an excited mess cook yelled down the gangway: "The Japs are bombing us and that's no s---!" Shirtless, Pond raced to man his gun.

All around him, Pearl Harbor was exploding. Within half an hour all seven of the battleships that lay on the southwest side of little Ford Island had been hit at least once by Japanese planes.

At Oahu's military airfields, mechanics and Marines with rifles were taking desperate pot shots at diving planes. At Ford Island's Naval Air Station, where almost half of the Navy's land-based planes were put out of commission in minutes, frantic flyers raced to get into the air in anything that still had wings. Only one ever succeeded in getting airborne.

Great greasy columns of smoke rose all around the harbor. The ancient minelayer *Oglala*, in dry dock on the south shore, simply "died of fright," as some eyewitnesses reported, her seams bursting open when a torpedo hit the cruiser *Helena*, berthed next to her. The destroyer *Shaw*, nearby, went up in a shower of rocketing ammunition *(right)* when a bomb hit her magazine; Seaman Ed Waszkiewicz, looking on from Ford Island, half a mile away, scrambled for cover when one of her shells landed near where he had been standing. Meanwhile, naval antiaircraft guns dotted the sky with explosive puffs (falling shrapnel did more damage to downtown Honolulu than Japanese bombs).

Well-rehearsed civilian volunteers came through magnificently. Provisional police directed traffic. Medical teams rushed to report for duty, some with no more warning than a radio announcer's shout: "This is the real McCoy!"

It was all too real. In two hours most of the U.S. Pacific Fleet had been put out of action, the Pacific air force shattered, thousands of men killed. And for America, the War had just begun.

The forward magazine of the United States destroyer Shaw explodes. Despite the violence of the blast, the ship stayed afloat, was repaired and sailed again.

Planes and hangars at the Ford Island Naval
Air Station go up in flame and smoke as
the attack continues. A wind sock at left
hangs limp, but the force of the blast in the
background billows a United States flag.
Despite the damage, ground defenses swung
swiftly into action; Navy Commander H. L.
Young, landing at Ford Island on a routine flight
from the carrier Enterprise, taxied in
with American bullet holes in his wings.

The hose-equipped garbage lighter YG-17
sprays sea water on the stricken West
Virginia. Though sunk in the shallow harbor,
the battleship remained upright when alert
crewmen counter-flooded her belowdecks as
she began listing heavily after torpedoes hit
below her waterline. YG-17's commander, Chief
Boatswain's Mate L. M. Jansen, also tried
vainly to put out the Arizona's fires.

A sailor dashes for cover amid the wreckage at the Kaneohe Bay Naval Air Station on Oahu's eastern coast. The dive bombers that plastered the base had already hit Pearl Harbor and Hickam Field but were still early enough to catch most of the men sleeping. One tired flyer was wakened by a mess cook who began beating a cake pan with a spoon.

The battleship California's crew swarms over her sides to the cry of "Abandon ship!" Oil from the burning Arizona at right has nearly engulfed the California's stern, still shaded by an awning rigged for church services. Similar canvas shades, which were stretched over her after guns, were torn by crewmen wielding kitchen knives in an attempt to clear the guns for action. At the extreme right is the capsized hull of the Oklahoma, where 415 entombed men drowned or suffocated before rescuers with acetylene torches could reach them.

vn antiaircraft guns set fire to the roof of the school.

Stretcher-bearers hurriedly carry a casualty to the temporary outdoor clinic at the Lunalilo Schoo

Household effects hastily pulled from burning homes during the attack clutter a quiet Oahu stree

A TERRIBLE TOLL IN SHIPS AND MEN

Rarely has the advantage of surprise in major warfare produced such dramatic and devastating losses. When the Japanese finally ceased their attack on Pearl Harbor, the toll for the United States was:

CASUALTIES—

Navy	2,008 killed	710 wounded
Marines	109 killed	69 wounded
Army	218 killed	364 wounded
Civilian	68 killed	35 wounded

Ships—

Lost: battleships *Arizona, Oklahoma;* target ship *Utah;* destroyers *Cassin, Downes*

Sunk or beached but salvageable: battleships *West Virginia, California, Nevada;* minelayer *Oglala*

Damaged: battleships *Tennessee, Maryland, Pennsylvania;* cruisers *Helena, Honolulu, Raleigh;* destroyer *Shaw;* seaplane tender *Curtiss;* repair ship *Vestal*

Aircraft—

Army

96 planes destroyed   128 planes damaged

Navy

92 planes destroyed   31 planes damaged

By contrast, out of a strike force of 31 ships and 353 raiding planes, the Japanese lost only 29 planes. In addition, one large submarine and five midget two-man subs, which had arrived in the Hawaii area earlier, were lost. Total deaths were 64 men, plus an unknown number of crew members aboard the large submarine.

The destroyers Cassin (right) and Downes lie half submerged in the shallow water by 1010 Dock, while smoke billows from Ford Island's Battleship Row in the distance. A bomb struck the Cassin's magazine, splintering her and badly damaging the Downes, which stayed afloat until a second missile struck both ships at once. The Pennsylvania, tied up behind them, got off with relatively light damage.

IN THE WAKE OF THE RAID

The wreckage of American planes amid the rubble of a hangar at Wheeler Field indicates the massive clean-up job facing survivors of the Pearl Harbor attack.

A BASTION FROM A BOMB-BLASTED ISLAND

When the last Japanese planes broke off their shattering assault on Pearl Harbor, they headed northwest to overtake carriers that were already speeding back to Japan. In the pattern of destruction left behind, survivors of the attack tended their wounded, battled the fires and counted their dead. Surrounded by wreckage and human suffering, they felt stranded and defenseless—"like you had four flat tires out in the desert," as one soldier put it.

Looming in their minds also was the threat of invasion—the pervasive fear the Japanese would follow their raid by landing on the islands. "They could have come in canoes and we couldn't have stopped them," said another soldier.

Invasion rumors and false reports were everywhere. Japanese paratroops were said to have landed on the big island of Hawaii. Word spread that Honolulu's water supply had been poisoned. The capture of the midget submarine at left escalated the invasion fears: perhaps it was on a reconnaissance mission to pave the way for landings.

The Hawaiians widely (and incorrectly) believed that a well-organized fifth column of spies and saboteurs existed among the island's large Japanese colony. Martial law was declared within hours of the raid. The FBI quickly rounded up suspected enemy agents, including 370 Japanese nationals, 98 Germans and 14 Italians. Against the possibility of further attacks, a total black-out was imposed on all of the Hawaiian Islands, and many servicemen's families were evacuated to the mainland. Gun emplacements and barbed wire bristled along mined beaches.

More importantly, as it turned out for the future course of the war, feverish and largely successful efforts were immediately instituted to salvage as much as possible of the battered Fleet. Of the 19 ships damaged by the bombing, all but three (the *Oklahoma*, *Utah* and *Arizona*) would see action later against the Japanese. Gradually, as rebuilding efforts accelerated, the reflexive fear and witch-hunting of the post-raid weeks receded, and Pearl Harbor and other Hawaiian bases were transformed into crucial staging areas for the eventual counterattack in the Pacific.

A Japanese midget sub that ran aground during the Pearl Harbor raid is displayed as a prize of war. The sub's pilot was the sole attacker captured.

The wife and son of a soldier stationed in Honolulu arrive in San Francisco aboard a ship carrying military dependents and other civilians to the mainland.

Strumming guitars and ukuleles, women of Oahu render traditional island songs—and "The Star Spangled Banner"—at the common grave of 328 U.S. Navy men killed at Pearl Harbor. Hundreds of mourners attended this touching memorial service at Nuuanu, near Honolulu, and heaped the grave with flowers. Several Japanese pilots who were shot down during the raid were buried here too. Their graves were ignored by everyone except one woman, who laid a bunch of flowers on one of the bare mounds with the remark: "They were some mothers' sons."

Civilian defense workers in Honolulu dig air-raid trenches in anticipation of further Japanese raids. Almost 10 miles of trenches were dug, in zigzag patterns designed to minimize casualties from single bombs.

To forestall epidemics of typhoid, diphtheria and smallpox, authorities inoculated approximately 350,000 islanders in the most extensive immunization program that had ever been attempted at a single location.

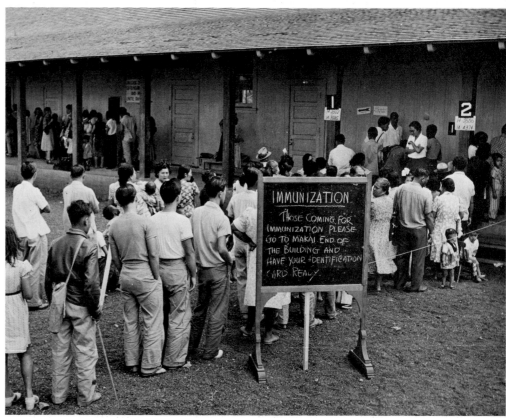

Navy wives and local women, hair covered as a sanitary precaution, roll bandages against a future assault. So many blood donors turned up—including the passengers and crew of a Dutch ship—they could barely be handled.

Gas masks are distributed at a Hawaiian school. Residents were required to carry masks at all times after the raid. Children's masks were specially padded; mothers were given gas bags into which babies could be popped.

Sailors on leave relax at Waikiki's posh Royal Hawaiian Hotel, taken over by the Navy after Pearl Harbor and used as a rest center by more than 200,000 men.

With Hawaii under martial law, a woman arrested for a speeding offense is sentenced by an Army officer to donate a pint of her blood. During the four years of military rule, such courts dispensed swift and often perceptive forms of justice, but public protests were sometimes aroused by the high-handed ways of the military authorities.

A sentry guards a Honolulu cable office against sabotage. By military fiat, cables and mail were censored; telephone calls to the United States or between islands were monitored and required to be in English. Newspapers were censored as well, and ad-libbed radio broadcasts were forbidden.

Less than a week after the Pearl Harbor raid, Army engineers erect the foundation for an underground hospital. At the same time, other engineers were strengthening coastal defenses and repairing runways so that fighters would be able to get into the air to combat new attackers.

A tin-hatted sailor chalks up morale-boosting messages from the top brass for all hands.

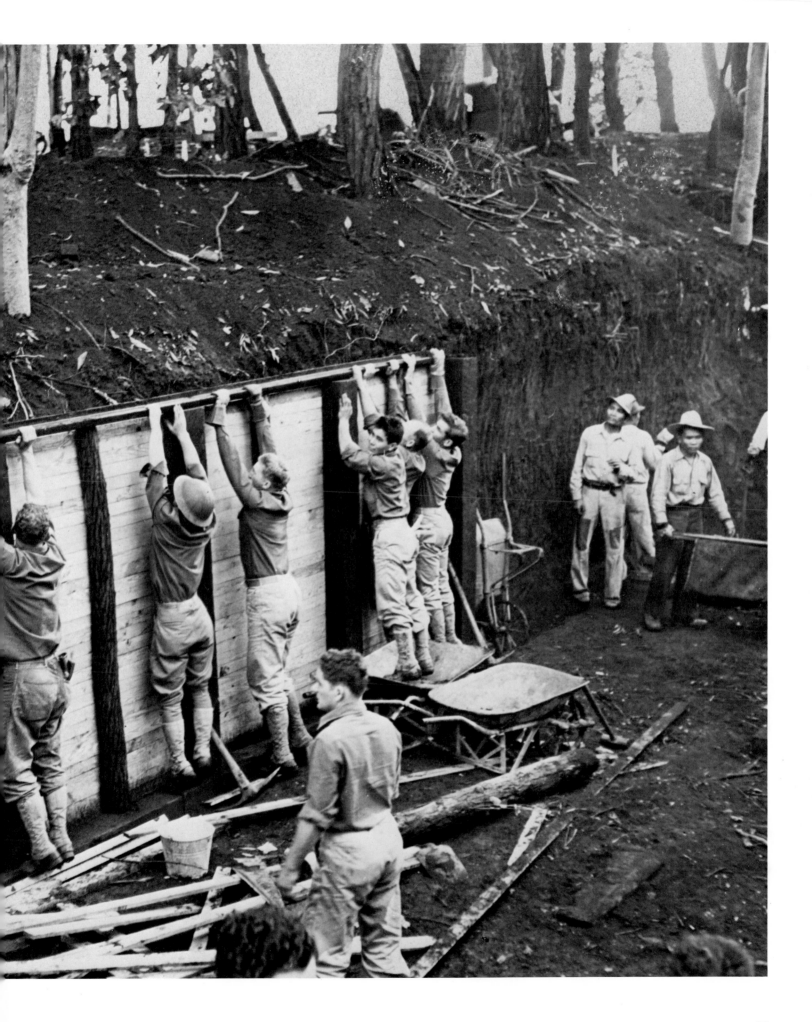

3

While the bombs rained down on Hawaii, Navy pilots of Japan's 11th Imperial Air Fleet, based on Formosa, spent a fitful night beside their planes, waiting for a heavy fog to lift. Their assignment: to bomb the critically important American airfields 500 miles away in the Philippines, part of a coordinated attack on United States possessions stretching across the Pacific Ocean from Pearl Harbor to Wake Island, Guam and Manila.

At 6 a.m., with the fog and tension on Formosa growing thicker by the hour, a loudspeaker crackled: "Attention! Here is an important announcement!" The news of the "devastating surprise attack" on Pearl Harbor sent the Japanese flyers into a whooping dance of celebration.

But now their mission had acquired an added risk. The Americans would no longer be surprised and would surely be waiting in strength to repulse any assault on the Philippines. Even worse, the delay that had been caused by the fog might well enable the aroused Americans to send their own bombers northward to catch the Formosa-based planes on the ground.

The fog lifted but the American raid never came. By 10:45 a.m. on December 8 (Philippine time) 108 Japanese bombers and 84 Zero fighters were airborne and speeding south toward Luzon, largest and northernmost of the Philippine Islands, certain that they would be met by an alert and vigorous defense. They were in for a pleasant surprise. "The sight that met us was unbelievable," related Saburo Sakai, a Zero pilot in the force attacking the main United States bomber base at Clark Field northwest of Manila. "Instead of encountering a swarm of American fighters diving at us in attack, we looked down and saw some sixty enemy bombers and fighters neatly parked along the airfield runways. They squatted there like sitting ducks."

As the Japanese bombers swept across the field at 22,000 feet, American antiaircraft fire blossomed up—thousands of feet too low. A few American fighters made it into the air, but they were too late. "The attack was perfect," Sakai recalled. "Long strings of bombs tumbled from the bays and dropped toward the targets. . . . The entire base seemed to be rising in the air with the explosions. Pieces of airplanes, hangars and other ground installations scattered wildly. Great fires erupted and smoke boiled upward."

Japanese fighters swooped down behind the bombers in

OUTPOSTS OVERWHELMED

savage strafing attacks. Sakai's own cannons chopped up two B-17 bombers on the runway. Then, as a parting shot, the Japanese pilot got an airborne American P-40 fighter in his sights and squeezed the trigger. Bullets crashed into the cockpit canopy, which blew off. "The fighter seemed to stagger," Sakai related, "then fell off and dived into the ground." It was the first kill of World War II for the man who was later to become the leading Japanese air ace to survive the conflict.

The attackers flew home, happy but bewildered. As the first Japanese bombers touched down on Formosa and the crews clambered out, one airman asked another, "What's the matter with the enemy? It seemed as though they did not know the war had started."

The enemy did know. General Douglas MacArthur, commander of U.S. Army Forces in the Far East, had received word of Pearl Harbor in his Manila Hotel suite at 3:30 a.m. (a warrant officer had heard the news while listening to a dance program on shortwave radio from the U.S. and had passed the word). By 5 a.m., Washington had confirmed the report and MacArthur had assembled his staff for a conference in his headquarters at No. 1, Calle Victoria.

MacArthur had been forewarned by Washington as early as November 27 of the possibility of an attack, and more recently Japanese aircraft had been spotted over Luzon. Although his intelligence officers doubted that Luzon was within striking range of the Japanese planes on Formosa, MacArthur had ordered his bomber force of 35 four-engine B-17s moved south from Clark Field to a less vulnerable new base in Mindanao. But any sense of urgency was as alien to the Philippines as it was to prewar Hawaii. When the war broke out, half the B-17s were still at Clark Field.

Immediately upon learning of the Japanese attack on Pearl Harbor, Major General Lewis Brereton, commander of the U.S. Army's air forces in the Philippines under MacArthur, had sought permission to launch his bombers against the Japanese airfields in Formosa. Brereton did not have adequate maps of Formosa, and he had no aerial reconnaissance photographs. His B-17s, also known as Flying Fortresses, were undergunned and slow and, because of the distance, would have to go in without fighter escort. But he felt that his crews could inflict some damage on the Japanese despite these drawbacks.

Brereton spoke to Major General Richard Sutherland, MacArthur's Chief of Staff throughout the Pacific war. For several hours, there was no answer to his request. As a precaution Brereton ordered his B-17s at Clark aloft with fighter cover. Then, shortly after 10 a.m., MacArthur gave Brereton the go-ahead to fly a photo reconnaissance mission to Formosa, which might be followed the next day by a bombing raid. Brereton called his planes in for refueling. It was then, at about 12:20 p.m., while the aircraft were lined up in neat rows and the crews were indoors eating lunch and studying what maps they had, that the Japanese bombers arrived over Clark Field and the American fighter base at nearby Iba.

The damage was devastating. All 18 of the B-17s were shot to bits, along with 53 P-40s and some 30 other aircraft; 80 servicemen were killed and 150 wounded. (Ironically, among the ground facilities destroyed was a radar system that could have given warning of the raid—except that it was not yet fully installed.) In the first hours of war, MacArthur had lost half of his air force.

Japan's program for conquest in the western Pacific and Southeast Asia had been launched with stunning effect. United States naval and air power in both Hawaii and the Philippines had been dealt a series of terrible blows. On the same day, the vital United States outposts at Guam and Wake were bombed, and invasions of those islands were sure to follow.

The objective of all these carefully-coordinated attacks was to cripple United States military power and establish a picket line of air and naval bases across the western Pacific behind which the Japanese could carry out a grandiose design. With the United States immobilized, the Japanese could march down through the Philippines, overrun Malaya and reduce the powerful British naval base at Singapore. When these attacks were well launched, they would be free to capture the Dutch East Indies, whose rich stores of oil were needed to fuel the Japanese war machine.

The first vital station along the Pacific picket line to fall into Japanese hands was Guam. The attack came while Pearl Harbor was still smoking, and Guam, a tiny Pan American Clipper stop 1,500 miles east of Manila in the Mariana Islands, was ill-prepared for war. In 1938 a special Navy

THE NIMBLE NEMESIS OF ALLIED FIGHTERS

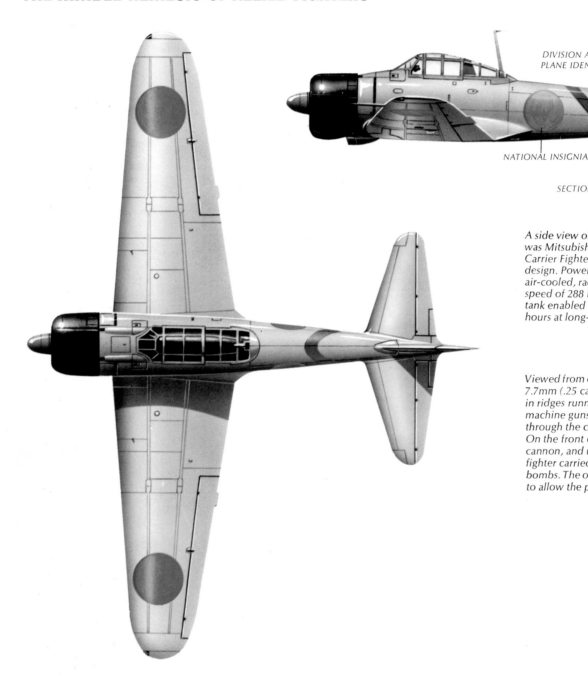

DIVISION AND
PLANE IDENTIFICATION — V-103

NATIONAL INSIGNIA

SECTION LEADER'S INSIGNIA

A side view of the Zero (its full official name was Mitsubishi A6M2 "Zero-Sen" Navy Type O Carrier Fighter Model 21) displays its clean design. Powered by a "Sakae 12" 14-cylinder, air-cooled, radial engine, the Zero had a top speed of 288 knots (331.5 mph). A reserve fuel tank enabled it to fly as long as six to eight hours at long-range cruising speeds.

Viewed from overhead, the Zero reveals its twin 7.7mm (.25 caliber) machine guns protruding in ridges running forward of the cockpit. The machine guns fired in synchronization through the circle of a three-blade propeller. On the front edge of each wing was a 20mm cannon, and under its wings and fuselage the fighter carried one 550- or two 130-pound bombs. The outer 18 inches of each wing folded to allow the plane to fit carrier elevators.

In the first few months of the Pacific war, an aura of invincibility developed around the Japanese Navy's single-seat Zero fighter. The frisky little plane chewed up Allied fighter opposition with contemptuous ease at Pearl Harbor. It brushed aside air opposition in the conquests of the Philippines, Malaya and the Dutch East Indies, causing havoc on the ground and scoring lopsided victories in the air.

The remarkably agile Japanese fighter was built of a light new aluminum alloy. Armor plating to protect the pilot and self-sealing gas tanks were sacrificed to give the Zero maximum speed and maneuverability. Powered by an engine that delivered only 950 hp, the light Zero could still outspeed and outrange most other fighters early in the war and outclimb any Allied plane then available in the Pacific.

But by 1943 the Zeroes were encountering new breeds of American fighter aircraft: P-38 Lightnings, F4U Corsairs and F6F Hellcats. Though less maneuverable at close range than the Zero, they could fly faster, were more durable and were more heavily armed. In addition, the new U.S. fighters were equipped with self-sealing tanks and with armor plating that afforded protection to the pilots. As a result, the new planes could close in on the Zero and slug it out at short range, where their superior firepower was fatally effective.

board had recommended, as part of a program to fortify United States outposts in the Pacific, that the island be developed into a first-rate air and submarine base. But Congress had refused to authorize the step, in part to avoid provoking the Japanese, who ironically were busily fortifying their own island possessions in the central Pacific.

On December 8, 1941, Guam was defended by a token garrison consisting of 427 Marines and Navy men plus 247 native troops. They were armed with no more than 170 rifles and a few World War I machine guns and Browning automatic rifles.

Guam's end was swift. In the hours after midnight on December 10, some 5,400 Japanese Marines and infantrymen splashed ashore. By dawn, they had reached the Governor's Palace, where a brief firefight took place. At 5:45 that morning, as the sun climbed out of the Pacific, three toots on an auto horn announced the American cease-fire. Navy Captain George McMillin, in command of the island, surrendered to a Japanese officer, who promptly ordered him to strip to his undershorts. On that ignominious note, the only piece of United States territory in the 3,000-mile stretch of the western Pacific between Wake Island and the Philippines was lost.

Wake was next. A lonely three-islet atoll about 2,300 miles west of Hawaii, Wake for most of its uneventful history was distinguished for little more than its roaring surf and its terns and frigate birds screaming overhead. Then, as war clouds gathered in 1941, the U.S. Navy, with the approval of Congress, belatedly began turning Wake into an air station—a kind of stationary aircraft carrier commanding the approaches to the southwestern Pacific. When Navy Commander Winfield Scott Cunningham arrived to take command of the atoll in November, he found a construction crew of 1,200 civilians hard at work building roads and landing strips and dredging a channel in the coral lagoon.

On the day the Japanese pulverized Pearl Harbor, there were 447 Marines on Wake, under Major James Devereux, along with some 75 Army Signal Corps and Navy personnel. The atoll's air protection consisted of a squadron of a dozen Marine fighter planes, under Major Paul Putnam. The Marine aviators flew Grumman Wildcats, which were slower and less maneuverable than the Japanese Zeroes. For artillery the Marines had three batteries of two 5-inch guns

each, and a dozen 3-inch antiaircraft guns. From scrub jungle thickets, machine guns guarded the beaches. There was no radar or dependable air-raid alarm system on the island (the Americans warned one another of incoming planes by firing three rifle shots in the air). Yet with this limited arsenal, Devereux's and Putnam's men were to hand the Japanese a stinging, if temporary, defeat.

The first attack on Wake occurred just before noon on Pearl Harbor Day. Upon hearing of the attack on Hawaii by radio, Devereux had his bugler sound "Call to Arms." The Marines grabbed their rifles; extra ammunition was trucked to the shore defense batteries and four of the short-range Grummans took off on patrol. Then a squall came up; the Grummans, patrolling at 12,000 feet, missed a flight of 36 enemy planes that winged in under the squall clouds from the Japanese-held atoll of Kwajalein 650 miles to the south. The Japanese planes bombed and strafed Wake's airstrip, blowing up seven of the eight United States planes still on the ground and damaging the other one. The Americans were left with only four operational fighters. With them, however, Putnam's pilots shot down half a dozen of the Japanese bombers that began making visits every day to soften up Wake's defenses.

Shortly after midnight on December 11, Marine lookouts saw blinking lights on the horizon, and by dawn a Japanese invasion force—consisting of three light cruisers, six destroyers, two patrol boats and two transports—was headed for Wake's coral reefs.

On orders from Commander Cunningham, the Marines manning the 5-inch guns held their fire as the Japanese pressed within range. At four miles offshore, the Japanese ships opened fire; still the Marines' guns were silent. Not until four of the Japanese warships were within 4,500 yards did the Americans begin firing. Almost immediately the 5-inchers, which had lost most of their fire-control equipment in the air raids, scored hits on two of the Japanese ships. The cruiser *Yubari,* flagship of the task force, limped away after being hit by three American shells. A destroyer, hit in an ammunition magazine, blew up and sank. At one battery, excited Marine gunners began shouting and jumping up and down until they were brought to their senses by a hardened platoon sergeant, Henry Bedell. "Knock it off, you bastards, and get back on the guns," he yelled. "What d'ya think this is, a ball game?"

That was not the last of the day's triumphs for the defenders of Wake. Another destroyer was hit, then a troop transport, a cruiser, and still another destroyer. The surviving Grummans did their share, dropping 100-pound bombs on the Japanese ships. Despite the fact that his plane was badly shot up by enemy antiaircraft fire, Captain Henry Elrod scored a direct hit on the depth charges stored on the afterdeck of the destroyer *Kisaragi,* and she blew up and sank with no survivors.

An incredible thing had happened. In a 45-minute battle a few hundred Marines had beaten off an entire Japanese invasion fleet. Without even attempting to land his assault troops, the Japanese commander, Rear Admiral Sadamichi Kajioka, turned his force around and sailed back toward Kwajalein. Two of his destroyers had been sunk and more than 500 of his men were dead. The Americans had lost only one man. "The eleventh day of December, 1941," historian Samuel Eliot Morison later wrote, "should always be a proud day in the history of the Corps." For the first time since the beginning of the war, the Japanese had been turned back. The attack on Wake Island, said one Japanese naval authority after the war, "was one of the most humiliating defeats our Navy ever suffered."

Cunningham, Devereux and their men were elated, but they knew that the Japanese would be back. Wake was too valuable a strategic outpost to be left in American hands. The air raids continued relentlessly and two hours after midnight on December 23 a second, larger invasion force under Admiral Kajioka arrived off Wake. This time it was supported by six heavy cruisers and two of the aircraft carriers that had attacked Hawaii, the *Soryu* and the *Hiryu.* Moreover, the invasion force included about 2,000 special naval landing troops—tough Japanese Marines.

The new assault was launched, Commander Cunningham later wrote, "in an atmosphere of desperate confusion from which only one clear factor emerged—the overwhelming numerical superiority of the invaders." About 1,000 Japanese Marines streamed ashore in the first wave. The American defenders were dispersed over the three little islands in small units. There were too few of them to cover all the beaches. Some of the civilian workers found weapons and fought side-by-side with the Marines. Others, unarmed, found what cover they could in foxholes and the brush.

The fighting was savage. On one island 70 Marines held off a landing force of 100 Japanese, killing almost every one of them. Yet in the confusion of battle it was reported to the American command post that the Japanese had overrun that sector. At dawn, dive bombers from the carriers pounded American positions on the atoll. There were no Wildcats to oppose them now; the last one had disappeared at sea the day before. But Major Putnam, Captain Elrod and the other survivors of the squadron took up rifles and fought until all but one of them was killed or wounded.

On the largest islet, the Japanese had reinforced the first assault wave and were putting increasing pressure on the Marines, who were pinned down by the heavy ground fire, bombing and strafing. Shortly after dawn one Japanese unit penetrated almost to an empty powder magazine that had been turned into a makeshift hospital and was crowded with American wounded.

At 7:30 a.m., the Marines were still holding on precariously, but Cunningham knew he was facing the inevitable. The island's defenders could probably last through the day, but once darkness set in they would surely be overrun. With more than 1,000 unprotected civilians on the island, the battle could become a massacre. After conferring with Devereux, Cunningham authorized the Marine major to surrender. Devereux reluctantly ordered the men around him to destroy their weapons and hoisted a bedsheet above his command bunker. Then, accompanied by a noncom who carried a white rag lashed to a mop handle, he set off down the road in search of the Japanese, directing his men to cease fire as he passed them along the way.

Wake Island fell two days before Christmas; 122 men died in its defense. The valor of its isolated defenders served to obscure a darker side of the Wake Island story: a sequence of events and decisions that were made many miles from that outpost.

The sad fact for the defenders was that two weeks before the final assault began, a naval task force had been ordered to reinforce Wake, but it was recalled before it reached the atoll. The task force included the 33,000-ton aircraft carrier Saratoga, carrying a total of 72 fighters and dive bombers and capable of a top speed of 34 knots. Commanded by Rear Admiral Frank Jack Fletcher, the task force got under way in time to help in the defense of Wake. But for more than three days Fletcher, characteristically cautious of his fuel supply, slogged along in the company of an oiler that could make no more than 13 knots.

At Pearl Harbor, following the relief of Admiral Kimmel, Vice Admiral William Pye was filling in temporarily as the commander in chief, Pacific Fleet. After the heavy losses of December 7, Pye was reluctant to risk the Saratoga, one of the only three large carriers available to the U.S. Pacific Fleet. At one point Pye ordered Fletcher to dash in and launch an air strike to help the defenders of Wake. Then he countermanded that order and directed Fletcher to send a seaplane tender ahead to evacuate the island. Later, he canceled that decision and ordered the task force home. No relief of any kind reached Wake.

Meanwhile, in the Philippines, the Japanese were preparing to heap more humiliation on the United States. In the week that followed the big raid on Clark Field, small Japanese forces landed on southeastern and northern Luzon. Recognizing these landings as diversionary attacks, MacArthur refused to commit his main ground forces. Instead, he sent planes from his greatly diminished force of P-40s and B-17s to attack the ships and transports.

One of the B-17s was piloted by Captain Colin Kelly Jr., who was to become America's first hero of the war. On December 10, Kelly made an audacious solo bombing run on what he and his crew thought was the Japanese battleship Haruna, north of Luzon. Smoke poured from the ship's stern and Kelly headed home to report a probable major sinking—dramatic news of a kind sorely needed by the embattled defenders of the Philippines and eagerly grasped by an American public still stunned by Pearl Harbor.

In fact, there were no battleships in Philippine waters that day and the vessel that Kelly attacked was probably a cruiser, which, if damaged at all, was not sunk.

Before Kelly could make it to Clark Field, his plane was jumped by Zeroes whose machine-gun and cannon fire riddled the bomber and set it on fire. Kelly crashed with his plane, but did keep it in the air just long enough for his six surviving crewmen to parachute to safety. He was awarded the Distinguished Service Cross posthumously, in part for heroically staying with his plane and in part because it was mistakenly believed he had sunk the Haruna.

The main Japanese attack in the Philippines was launched at dawn on December 22, when 43,000 troops of Lieut. General Masaharu Homma's 14th Army waded ashore on the palm-fringed beaches of Lingayen Gulf, 120 miles north of Manila. Homma's divisions were tested by combat in China and well supported by armor and artillery. Homma himself was a veteran of the China campaigns. Imperial General Headquarters had allotted him 50 days to take Luzon.

General MacArthur, as commander of the combined U.S. and Philippine Army forces, could field almost three times as many troops as General Homma. But they included 100,000 raw Philippine reservists, who were lightly trained, poorly equipped and indifferently led. MacArthur had spent the immediate prewar years trying to help the Philippines organize an effective armed force in anticipation of the commonwealth's becoming fully independent by 1946. But there was no sense of urgency and progress had been slow.

The captured Marine commander of Wake Island, Major James P. Devereux (center) and fellow prisoners at a Shanghai prisoner-of-war camp hold radios presented to them by the Japanese camp commander. The Japanese normally forbade radios in POW camps—sometimes on pain of death. The ones that were given to Devereux and his comrades were fixed to receive only Japanese broadcasts. This picture of the presentation was used in a Japanese propaganda magazine.

The pride of his command were the Philippine Division of the U.S. Army (which included the 31st Infantry Regiment, made up wholly of Americans) and some 12,000 Scouts, Filipino members of the U.S. Army who were to prove themselves fierce and indomitable defenders of their homeland. One division of the regular Philippine Army was in fighting shape and the 4th Regiment, U.S. Marines, had arrived in November from Shanghai. In all, MacArthur could count on only 25,000 to 30,000 reliable regulars.

Homma's invasion was opposed by the Northern Luzon Force, under the American Major General Jonathan Wainwright. A few Philippine Army units under his command fought bravely, but they were quickly overwhelmed. The rest of them crumbled and fled. By nightfall, tank-led columns were rolling toward Manila, and the Northern Luzon Force was in full retreat.

Hardly were General Homma's troops ashore at Lingayen Gulf when another Japanese amphibious force struck Luzon's Lamon Bay, about 70 miles southeast of Manila. The two Japanese columns thus formed a pincer closing in on the capital city. In the north, General Wainwright attempted, on Christmas Day, 1941, to set up a defensive line behind the natural barrier of the Agno River. But the crack Japanese 48th Division, with its artillery and tanks, quickly broke through and by the evening of December 26, Wainwright's army was again in retreat.

MacArthur had foreseen what was coming and, as early as December 23, had decided to revive an old but long-shelved contingency plan: to pull back all his forces on Luzon into Bataan, a 30-mile peninsula of wooded mountains, dense jungle and precipitous ravines separating Manila Bay from the South China Sea. This move would leave Manila to Homma's troops but the American and Filipino troops could deny them the use of its harbor from the island fortress of Corregidor at the entrance to Manila Bay. "He may have the bottle, but I have the cork," said MacArthur. For the tactic to succeed, Wainwright's troops would have to hold off the Japanese in the north long enough for Major General George Parker's Southern Luzon Force, which had vigorously opposed the landings southeast of Manila, to retreat past the capital into Bataan.

The Army's transport units had not nearly enough trucks to carry out such a withdrawal, so Manila's gaudily painted buses were pressed into service, carrying load after load of soldiers, food and ammunition into the peninsula. Seldom has a military retreat assumed a more bizarre look: the brightly colored buses and olive-drab army vehicles mingled in immense traffic jams with the cars and wooden oxcarts of Philippine civilians fleeing the Japanese.

As his army retreated toward Bataan, MacArthur was preparing to move his headquarters to Corregidor, where the Philippine Commonwealth government of President Manuel Quezon would join him.

At sundown on a cheerless Christmas Eve, the general, his staff, his wife Jean, their four-year-old son Arthur and the boy's Cantonese nursemaid, Ah Cheu, gathered on the dock below the Manila Hotel. As dinner music floated out from the hotel's ballroom, the party boarded the inter-island steamer Don Esteban for the 22-mile journey to the island called The Rock.

From beyond the waterfront came the rumble of explosions as supplies of fuel and other stores were destroyed to prevent them from falling into Japanese hands. At Cavite Navy Yard to the south of Manila a million barrels of oil were put to the torch and great tongues of flame rose in the darkened sky. Aboard the steamer, MacArthur sat alone, head in hands. Someone started singing "Silent Night" and one by one the others joined in.

MacArthur ordered General Parker to Bataan to start preparing the peninsula's defense. In the week that followed, General Wainwright and Parker's successor, Major General Albert Jones, fought a delaying action toward Bataan, finally getting the last guns and trucks of the South Luzon Force across the Pampanga River early on New Year's Day and dynamiting its bridges a few hours ahead of the advancing Japanese. By January 6, most—but not all—of MacArthur's army on Luzon had crossed the river into Bataan. Several small detachments, cut off during the retreat, dispersed into the hills and jungle to form guerrilla bands. Thousands of Filipino reservists simply stopped being soldiers and went home.

The Japanese occupied Manila on January 2. That evening, a Japanese color guard assembled beneath the sprawling acacia trees on the lawn of the residence of the United States High Commissioner. A Japanese Marine hauled down

Deep inside Malinta Tunnel (above), on Corregidor, the U.S. Army headquarters staff directs Bataan's defense. Corregidor fell at the climax of a campaign launched with an attack on Clark Field (below). Landing on northern Luzon, the Japanese fought their way down through Bataan. The capture of Corregidor completed the five-month campaign.

the Stars and Stripes and ground it under his heel. As the band played "Kimigayo," the Japanese national anthem, sunset guns boomed a salute and the Marine ran up the Rising Sun. On Homma's orders, British and American civilians were rounded up for internment but otherwise they were not harmed.

Meanwhile, some 15,000 American and 65,000 Filipino troops were digging in on Bataan. They were faced with a grim situation. Bataan's stock pile of rations was sufficient to feed 100,000 people for a month and the peninsula was jammed with 80,000 troops and 26,000 cilivian refugees. The supply of ammunition was insufficient for a protracted siege. Worst of all, perhaps, medicine was in short supply, especially quinine, the only remedy for malaria at that time. Bataan, with its steaming jungles and mosquitoes, was a fertile ground for malaria. Soon, soldiers by the thousands were down with chills and fever.

The remaining B-17s had been evacuated to Australia and the small U.S. Asiatic Fleet had withdrawn to Java.

For the defense of Bataan, MacArthur deployed his forces in a 20-mile line across the upper neck of the peninsula. One corps, under Wainwright, held the tangled, precipitous western coast. The other, which was commanded by Parker, stretched to the swampy eastern shore. Separating them was 4,200-foot Mount Natib, whose steep, wooded slopes and snarled, nearly impassable gullies made it impossible to establish effective contact between the two corps.

The Japanese, believing that Bataan would soon be theirs, removed General Homma's best division, the 48th, for use in the planned invasion of Java. In its place, from Formosa, came the 65th Brigade, made up mostly of conscripts with barely a month's training.

The Japanese offensive began on January 9 with a concentrated artillery barrage that shook the northern end of the peninsula. Parker's position on the western half of Bataan came under attack first. On January 11 in the evening— a time favored for attack by the Japanese—infantrymen yelling "Banzai!" charged the barbed wire that protected the American and Filipino lines. Some of the attacking soldiers threw themselves onto the wire, making bridges of corpses that the men of the second wave could scramble across. But the first attack was thrown back at a cost to the Japanese of 300 dead.

Two weeks of hard fighting ensued all along the front with temporary successes for both sides. Tanks and artillery were employed by both armies, but the Japanese had complete control of the air. Finally two of Homma's best regiments, advancing down the center of the peninsula along the slopes of Mount Natib, turned the inner flanks of Wainwright's and Parker's corps and threatened to cut off their avenue of retreat.

MacArthur ordered a withdrawal to a new line halfway down the peninsula. The retreat was badly disorganized, with soldiers scrambling over rocky beaches and clambering through jungle ravines. The few roads in the region were jammed with battered buses and trucks and exhausted soldiers. As the men of an American rear guard staggered into new positions on January 25, bearded and unwashed, their uniforms in shreds, one of their officers studied their faces. They "lacked any semblance of expression," he wrote later; the soldiers looked "like walking dead men."

Even as they fell back, the Americans encountered a new threat to their rear. The Japanese made four amphibious landings at narrow points of land in the southwest corner of Bataan. These areas were lightly defended by a polyglot combination of Service Command troops: sailors, Marines, airmen who had lost their planes, and Philippine Constabulary. Prompt reinforcement of the threatened areas by the hard-fighting Filipino Scouts contained the landings and gradually the Japanese were driven back to the beaches. At one point, the Japanese holed themselves up in cliffside caves at the water's edge; eventually they were annihilated by fire from Navy PT boats offshore and sticks of dynamite tossed down by the Scouts from above. The Americans were learning a lesson that was to be repeated many times in the Pacific war: the Japanese soldier, no matter how desperate his position, preferred death to surrender.

By mid-February the amphibious threat had been erased. But at the new defense line, the Japanese had paused hardly at all before hitting hard at Parker's forces on the east and Wainwright's on the west, hoping to break through before the defenders could dig in. In the dim light of the nearly impenetrable jungle, the battle became a close-range infantry dual. One Japanese regiment managed to slip through Wainwright's overextended front, but was then trapped by American-Filipino counterattacks. Forming a circular defensive position, the Japanese fought back desperately. But Wainwright's men broke them into two pockets and gradually wiped out one of the encircled groups. The Japanese colonel leading the other group managed to fight his way back through the jungle to his own lines with some of his men. But, of the 1,000 men who had broken through Wainwright's front two weeks earlier, only 377 survived.

The stiffness of the resistance convinced Homma by the second week in February that he should call off the offensive. He had used up more than the 50 days allotted him to conquer Luzon, and had lost more than 7,000 dead and wounded in the fighting on Bataan. Another 10,000 to 12,000 were down with malaria, dengue fever, dysentery or beriberi. Yet his stubborn foe still held half the peninsula. Homma pulled his exhausted army back a few miles and asked Tokyo for reinforcements. During the lull of nearly two months that followed, the United States and Philippine troops strengthened their position, laying minefields and reorganizing their remaining artillery.

But by this time the main enemy was no longer the Japanese. Sickness and malnutrition were gradually paralyzing MacArthur's army. The quinine supply had almost completely run out, and food supplies were so low that the men in the trenches looked like walking skeletons.

The Japanese at this point were not strong enough to resume their offensive, but they introduced a new element of terror into the campaign by resorting to unconventional tactics. Infiltrating by ones and twos, they reassembled in units of up to platoon strength at predetermined points in the jungle well behind the American-Filipino lines. From there they raised havoc with the rear echelons, ambushing patrols, burning supplies, and stealing food and weapons. Soldiers bivouacked in supposedly secure camps frequently woke in the morning to find that men next to them had been stabbed to death in their sleep. Anyone who was unfortunate enough to be captured by the Japanese could expect to be executed.

Morale, which had risen almost feverishly when the Japanese offensive was halted, began a steady descent toward despair. The inroads of hunger, disease and incessant air raids were compounded by a sense of growing hopelessness. A radio address by President Roosevelt on February

The commander of U.S. Army Forces in the Far East, General Douglas MacArthur, confers with President Manuel Quezon of the Philippines on Corregidor as the Philippine campaign approaches its climax. Shortly before his nation was occupied, Quezon left by submarine for Australia, and later went to the United States to set up a government in exile. MacArthur departed by PT boat for Mindanao, then flew to Australia, where he established a new headquarters.

23, intended to inspire the troops, served mainly to clarify the grimness of their situation by emphasizing that there was no hope of reinforcement from the United States.

Meanwhile MacArthur, relatively safe on fortified Corregidor, became known derisively to his starving men as Dugout Doug, and his departure for Australia at this point did little to endear him to his men.

MacArthur had been prepared to stay to the end, to be taken prisoner or die on Corregidor. For weeks he had resisted pressure from Washington to leave the Philippines. Then in late February, Roosevelt personally ordered him to Australia to assume command of American forces that were to assemble there for an eventual counteroffensive. On March 10 MacArthur summoned Wainwright, told him of

the departure order and assigned him to command the forces on Luzon. "If I get through to Australia," MacArthur said, "I'll come back as soon as I can with as much as I can."

The next evening MacArthur, his family and some of his staff went aboard four motor-torpedo boats rocking alongside Corregidor's broad concrete pier. On board PT-41, MacArthur turned to the skipper, Lieutenant John Bulkeley, a bearded, barrel-chested young officer with twin pistols on his hips, who had sunk two landing craft in the ill-fated Japanese amphibious attack on Bataan. "You may cast off, Buck, when you are ready," MacArthur said. He raised his cap in salute to those on shore as the boats slid away through Corregidor's minefields toward open sea.

MacArthur and his party went by boat to Mindanao, 500

miles to the south. From there, he transferred to a B-17 for the 1,600-mile flight to Darwin.

Shortly after his arrival in Australia, while crossing the continent by train to Melbourne, the general received a message from U.S. Army Chief of Staff, General George C. Marshall, telling him that no American infantry divisions, and no tanks or heavy weapons, had yet been dispatched to Australia. MacArthur also discovered that the 250 Allied planes in Australia were rapidly being shot up by the Japanese. Australia itself was in such danger of invasion that two Australian divisions were being called home from the Middle East. The impact of this gloomy intelligence punctured even MacArthur's persistent optimism. "God have mercy on us," he murmured.

Nevertheless, an hour after he had been briefed on the situation, MacArthur went before news reporters and read a short, toughly worded statement. He had come to Australia, he said, to organize "the American offensive against Japan." He concluded with a pledge that was to become the battle cry of the Allied effort. "I came through," MacArthur said, "and I shall return."

Before leaving the Philippines, MacArthur had reorganized his command into four parts, all to be responsible to him in Australia through an advance headquarters on Corregidor. But Washington, unaware of this, named Wainwright commander of all United States forces in the Philippines. On March 20, after some embarrassing confusion, Wainwright assumed overall command and was promoted to lieutenant general. MacArthur retained "supervisory" responsibility from Australia.

Meanwhile the agony of Bataan went on. By the end of March, barely a fourth of the original 80,000 defenders were combat-effective. And most of these were sick, or on the edge of starvation. A thousand men a day were falling out with malaria. Rations, which had already been cut in half and then cut again, now consisted of but eight to 10 ounces of rice a day plus an ounce or two of fish or canned meat. In some instances officers had to restrain their men from eating rotting chunks of dead animal flesh.

Washington was making an effort to resupply the Philippine garrison, but the results were pitifully inadequate. Japan's Army had seized key bases in the southern Philippines. Its Navy patrolled the narrow sea lanes from Australia and the Dutch East Indies. Despite elaborate and sometimes heroic efforts to run the blockade, only three supply ships reached the Philippines. An occasional submarine carrying food or ammunition surfaced at Mindanao or Corregidor, but for the most part the Battling Bastards of Bataan, as they called themselves, were on their own.

At the same time, the Japanese were revitalizing their forces in Bataan. General Homma's riddled 14th Army was reinforced with 21,000 fresh troops, some 150 new field guns and 60 bombers. Homma himself remained in command despite the reverses suffered by his army, but Tokyo displayed its impatience with his lack of progress by replacing three of his senior staff officers.

On the morning of April 3, the stalemate on Bataan suddenly ended. The day had a special significance for each of the opposing armies. For those on one side of the line it was Good Friday; for those on the other side it was the anniversary of the death of the legendary Emperor Jimmu, ancestor of Hirohito.

The Japanese preceded their attack with a devastating five-hour air and artillery bombardment, the heaviest of the campaign thus far. The pounding was followed immediately by a massive assault of armor and infantry against the center of the American line. Dazed and disorganized by the ferocity of the attack, the Americans and Filipinos fell back, resisted, then retreated again. On Saturday the bombardment was renewed, scorching the jungle and turning carefully prepared defenses into twisted wreckage. By Easter Sunday the Japanese had stormed their first objective—the upper slopes of 1,900-foot Mount Samat, which provided a commanding view of the battlefield below. Two Philippine Army divisions had been obliterated and General Parker's corps was in danger of being driven into Manila Bay.

The next day Major General Edward King Jr., who had taken command on Bataan when Wainwright replaced MacArthur on Corregidor, threw most of his slim reserve, including the prized 31st Infantry, into a desperate counterattack. But the emaciated and outgunned Americans were no match for the Japanese. By nightfall the trails and crude roads to the south were clogged with thousands of Americans and Filipinos staggering away from the front. Japanese tanks and infantry pressed on their heels and Zeroes swept in unmolested on deadly strafing runs.

As the front crumbled, United States demolition teams at Mariveles, on Bataan's southern tip, began blowing up the remaining ammunition stock piles and setting fuel supplies afire. Some 2,000 persons, including 104 nurses, managed to escape to Corregidor by small boat and barge. From Corregidor, Wainwright, under explicit orders from MacArthur, ordered a final counterattack. But King, in the field, decided against it.

At 11 a.m. on April 9—six days after the final Japanese offensive began—King sat down at a field table across from General Homma's operations officer, Colonel Motoo Nakayama. The American general asked for a 12-hour stay to collect his wounded. Nakayama coldly refused. "Will our troops be well treated?" King asked. Nakayama assured him: "We are not barbarians." Wearily, King unstrapped his sidearm, laid it on the table and surrendered the remaining 76,000 men on Bataan.

On Corregidor, MacArthur's successor still held the cork. The island's Malinta Tunnel, an elaborate network of bombproof underground passages reinforced with concrete, was fitted out as a combination staff headquarters, communications center, ammunition dump, hospital and bomb shelter. Coastal guns and mortars, 56 in all, were supplemented by even larger 14-inch guns on three nearby islands. One of these islands, Fort Drum, resembled an oversized pillbox, bristling with 14-inch and 6-inch guns; it was nicknamed "the concrete battleship." The Japanese now turned all of their power against the fortified islands.

The outcome was never in doubt. For nearly a month the 13,000 Americans and Filipinos on Corregidor were subjected to an almost continuous artillery barrage. Day and night, shells from more than 100 Japanese guns crashed down. So intense was the bombardment that survivors said it seemed as though giant machine guns were firing at them instead of cannons. Fires raged over the surface of the island until it was little more than a blackened cinder. The fissures in Malinta Tunnel's concrete walls widened under the pounding. Dust, dirt and the stench of death were everywhere. One by one The Rock's own guns—most of them in open emplacements vulnerable to air bombardment and high-angle shelling—fell silent.

Fatigue, hunger and the terror of the endless bombardment exacted their toll. "Constant exposure to gunfire, destruction and death altered our sense of values drastically," wrote one survivor. "We asked only to live from day to day. A full meal, a bath, a chance to sleep under a bombproof roof—these were the essentials."

On May 2, Corregidor's last big gun emplacement took a direct hit in its magazine. Ten-ton mortar barrels flew into the air like matchsticks; exploding ammunition shook the rocky fortress. Now only the guns of Fort Drum—the concrete battleship—were responding effectively to the Japanese barrage. Three nights later, Homma's troops landed on Corregidor. Within four hours they were only a mile away from the mouth of Malinta Tunnel. Tanks rolled ashore, and Japanese artillery zeroed in on the last American line of defense, manned in part by 500 sailors who were fighting as infantrymen.

Shortly before noon on May 6, Wainwright cabled President Roosevelt: "With broken heart, and head bowed in sadness but not in shame, I report to Your Excellency that today I must arrange terms for the surrender of the fortified islands of Manila Bay." He radioed MacArthur in Australia: "I have fought for you to the best of my ability from Lingayen Gulf to Bataan to Corregidor. Goodbye, General."

But it was a young Army radio operator, Corporal Irving Strobing, from Brooklyn, who tapped out Corregidor's last message: "Everyone is bawling like a baby. They are piling dead and wounded in our tunnel. . . . The jig is up."

Under a white flag, Wainwright went ashore to meet Homma, who insisted that he surrender not only Corregidor but the entire Philippines. Wainwright agonized over the decision—the United States and Filipino commands in Mindanao and other islands had not been defeated and were prepared to fight on, as guerrillas if necessary. But Homma made it clear that there would be no cease-fire unless all the forces were surrendered. Because he was convinced that Malinta Tunnel, with its nurses, its wounded and its terrified civilians, would become a slaughterhouse, Wainwright capitulated. The next day, by Japanese radio from Manila, he instructed the commanders of all units in the Philippines to follow suit. Reluctantly, over the next five weeks, they did so one by one, but not before several thousand of their troops had vanished into the hills, to survive, and resist, as best they could.

TRAGEDY IN THE PHILIPPINES

To spare his exhausted, defeated men, Major General Edward King (center) arranges with a Japanese colonel the surrender of the Philippine bastion of Bataan.

A NIGHTMARE WORSE THAN SURRENDER

On April 9, 1942, the 76,000 Filipino and American troops on Bataan yielded to the Japanese the mountainous peninsula they had held for 14 weeks. The surrender marked the largest capitulation by a United States military command in history. A month later the 13,000 defenders of Corregidor gave up their rocky island at the entrance of Manila Bay. Except for scattered guerrilla resistance, the fall of the Philippines was complete.

For the beaten troops, surrender was the beginning of a nightmare of captivity. The Corregidor prisoners were given no food for a week, then hauled ashore in freighters and driven like cattle through the streets of Manila to celebrate the Japanese triumph. Finally they were shipped by train to an improvised prison camp at Cabanatuan.

The fate of Bataan's survivors was even worse. The Japanese, expecting some 25,000 reasonably healthy captives, were confronted with more than twice that number of men, most of them sick and starving. Food, water and medicines quickly ran short. Far too few trucks and trains had been allotted to haul the prisoners 65 miles north to Camp O'Donnell. For most captives the trip became a footslogging endurance test. Some Japanese treated prisoners well, sharing food and cigarettes with the marchers and even releasing prisoners they had been ordered to kill. But most of the captors regarded surrender as an unforgivable offense and prisoners as unworthy of any consideration. They clubbed, stabbed and shot helpless stragglers and in one bloody two-hour orgy bayoneted and beheaded some 350 Filipino soldiers. Some guards forced captives to bury stricken comrades alive, even as they struggled feebly to escape from their newly-dug graves.

Of the 70,000 men who were able to begin the Death March, at least 7,000 died. The rest, said an American doctor who survived, made it to imprisonment at Camp O'Donnell "on the marrow of their bones." A soldier-poet who would later die in captivity wrote of Bataan's benumbed marchers: *The suffering column moves. I leave behind/Only another corpse, beside the road.*

Flanked by a Japanese censor, General Wainwright, United States Philippines commander, broadcasts a surrender order after Corregidor's fall.

Filipino and American troops give up outside Corregidor's 1,400-foot Malinta Tunnel, in which their garrison withstood 27 days of artillery bombardment.

Filipino and American soldiers are disarmed by their conquerors at Mariveles before the start of the Bataan Death March. Many captives were also stripped of food, watches and other valuables. One prisoner, a former Notre Dame football player, lost his 1935 class ring to a guard but it was returned by a Japanese officer who politely explained: "I graduated from Southern California in 'thirty-five."

Exhausted troops of the Corregidor garrison lie with their feet propped up on shoes to improve blood circulation. These men were taken from their fortress by freighter, then crammed into oven-like steel boxcars for a four-hour trip to Cabanatuan, an unfinished Philippine Army camp. By the end of the first two months of captivity there, 2,000 Americans had died of hunger and disease.

Hands tied behind their backs, captives Samuel Stenzler, Frank Spear and James Gallagher rest briefly during a halt on the exhausting trip to prison camp.

Shouldering improvised litters bearing their disabled comrades, Bataan marchers approach the end of their arduous journey—the prison enclosure at Camp

O'Donnell, on a dusty plain in Luzon. There, malaria, dysentery, malnutrition and brutality claimed the lives of up to 400 Americans and Filipinos a day.

THE DOOLITTLE RAID

Before their historic surprise raid on Japan, the crew of the B-25 piloted by the strike's leader, Lieut. Colonel Doolittle (second from left), line up beside the plane.

BOMBERS THAT BLASTED JAPANESE CONFIDENCE

Ever since the 13th Century, when a typhoon demolished an invading Mongol armada, the Japanese people had believed that a *Kamikaze*, or Divine Wind, made their island nation invulnerable. In 1942 that belief was buttressed by a modern confidence in naval air and sea patrols. But on April 18 of that year, both beliefs were shattered when 16 U.S. Army bombers, led by Lieut. Colonel James H. Doolittle, swept in from the sea to bomb Tokyo and four other major Japanese cities, then vanished westward as swiftly as they came.

Planning for this bold thrust began soon after the United States debacle at Pearl Harbor, with the dual aim of denting Japanese confidence and boosting American morale. But Japan was beyond the reach of any land-based U.S. bombers, and an attack by regular carrier-based planes with their limited 300-mile range would be suicidal; Japanese air and sea forces would blow the U.S. carriers out of the water before they could get close enough to launch their aircraft.

The solution was unique: to launch land-based B-25 bombers from a carrier cruising beyond the normal radius of Japanese patrols. Amid tight security, a Navy pilot taught short-takeoff techniques to hand-picked Army airmen. They learned their destination only after they were aboard the carrier *Hornet*, whose decks were packed with lashed-down B-25s. After 18 days at sea, laden with bombs and extra fuel tanks, the B-25s staggered into the air from the *Hornet's* pitching flight deck some 700 miles from Tokyo. Picket boats had spotted the carrier, but while the Japanese waited for her to come within normal launching range, the bombers zoomed in to drop their loads on the soil of Japan. Then, unscathed by disorganized ground and air attacks, the B-25s flew toward sanctuaries in Russia and China.

Though the brief foray did no great damage, it did help to change the course of the war. Haunted by the fear of another attack, the Japanese rashly accelerated plans for extending their defense perimeter, a decision that led within weeks to a costly defeat in the Battle of Midway. The raid also affected ordinary citizens. "We started to doubt," one of them later recalled, "that we were invincible."

As Doolittle's lead plane dissolves into a speck in the distance, the second Japan-bound B-25 lifts off from the spray-swept deck of the U.S.S. Hornet.

Aboard the Hornet before takeoff, a bomber crew preparing to repel possible attack by enemy fighters over Japan loads .50-caliber machine-gun ammunition.

The naval base at Yokosuka in Tokyo Bay appears beneath the propeller hub of the starboard engine of a B-25 copiloted by Richard A. Knobloch, a 23-year-old lieutenant from Milwaukee, Wisconsin. Seconds after snapping the picture with his pocket camera, Knobloch watched in fascination as four 500-pound American bombs blasted workshops, a floating dry dock in which a merchantman was being converted into an aircraft carrier, and other installations. Virtually all other photographs taken during the raid were lost when all but one of the 16 planes, their fuel gone or nearly exhausted, either crash-landed in China or were abandoned in mid-air. The pilot of the other bomber, forced by a leaking gas tank to decide between ditching off the China coast or seeking the nearest friendly land—Siberia—chose to land in Vladivostok, where the Russians interned the crew and impounded the plane and all cameras.

Doolittle surveys the wreckage of his bomber, which crashed in a Chinese rice paddy after the crew had parachuted to safety.

In sedan chairs carried by friendly Chinese, a B-25 crew heads for the Chinese capital, Chungking, to join other downed raiders.

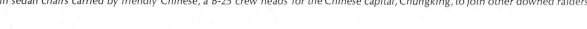

Resting safely at a home in Chuchow after their landing in China, American airmen—one of them taking his ease in bed—welcome a delegation of Chinese.

After having parachuted into China only two miles from Japanese occupation forces, these four American flyers pause in their escape from searching enemy troops and planes—which they managed to elude with the assistance of Chinese farmers and soldiers. In accomplishing their flight, the airmen used almost every type of Chinese conveyance—river boat, pony, ricksha, sedan chair, and charcoal-burning bus and train.

A bomber crew is feted at a farewell celebration at a Chinese coastal village before departing for Chungking. To retaliate against the Chinese for rescuing and harboring the Americans, the Japanese launched a ruthless three-month reign of terror, slaughtering thousands of Chinese civilians and laying waste entire towns and villages.

Lieutenant Robert Hite (left), one of eight flyers captured by the Japanese in occupied China, is led blindfolded from a transport plane in Tokyo. Three of the eight were executed and another died in prison. Hite and his surviving companions endured 40 months of mostly solitary imprisonment, until Japan's defeat ended their ordeal.

Lieut. General Tomoyuki Yamashita, the hard-bitten commander of Japan's 25th Army, was not a man normally given to poetry. But in the early hours of December 4, 1941, as 19 transports loaded with troops of his command steamed out of harbor on the morning tide, Yamashita glanced at the sky and saw that though the sun was up, the moon had not yet set. Their joint presence struck him as a fine omen. On an impulse, standing outside his cabin aboard the *Ryujo Maru,* he composed a short poem to mark the moment.

Somehow, Yamashita's devoted aides failed to preserve his poetic effort for posterity, but his hunch that good fortune impended was to prove spectacularly accurate. For the next six months, success after success would attend the far-flung military ventures now being set in motion. The objective of these ambitious undertakings was no less than the total takeover of Southeast Asia.

By now, Indochina was in Japanese hands, occupied in 1941 with the abject consent of a fallen France. The strategy being initiated by Yamashita and his troops called for the occupation of Thailand, coupled with a sweep down through the jungle-covered Malay Peninsula to capture the British stronghold at Singapore. Meanwhile, massive Japanese air and naval forces would launch a major assault against the oil-rich Dutch East Indies; then the Japanese could cap their military adventures in Southeast Asia by driving the British out of strategically vital Burma.

From Yamashita's starting point, the island of Hainan off the southern coast of China, a distance of 1,100 miles of open sea would have to be covered before his invasion armada reached its destination. The convoy was heading for three small fishing ports on the east shore of the Kra Isthmus, the narrow neck of land where southern Thailand bordered northern Malaya. In all, the war planners in Tokyo had estimated, the journey would take four days.

Yamashita's convoy would steam down across the South China Sea, and rendezvous with an escort of Japanese warships off the southern tip of Indochina. The combined force would then enter the Gulf of Siam, veering off sharply to the west and south until it arrived at the projected invasion beaches on the far side of the gulf.

A hint of the remarkable luck that was to favor Yamashita's expedition came shortly after noon on December 6. The rendezvous had just been effected when a Hudson bomber,

4

THE STRIKE TO THE SOUTH

on patrol from the British air base at Kota Bharu in northern Malaya, appeared out of the clouds. The pilot did not tarry; he was at the outermost limits of his range. Back at base he reported what he had seen: a number of ships—merchant ships, apparently—accompanied by Japanese cruisers and destroyers. Some, he said, were traveling northwest, others west, still others southward.

The report, relayed 350 miles down the Malay Peninsula to British Far East Command headquarters in Singapore, was duly pondered. That the Japanese were on the move was evident—but moving where? Possibly Bangkok, or Singora, a port in southern Thailand not far from the frontier with Malaya. Or northern Malaya itself, near Kota Bharu. Or, possibly, all three places.

If the target lay in Thailand, the British would be faced with a delicate situation. Of all Southeast Asia's countries, Thailand alone had managed to avoid becoming an appendage of some far-off imperial power. The British in Malaya had worked out a plan, under the code name of *Matador*, for sending troops to the defense of Singora, if a Japanese invasion of southern Thailand appeared imminent. But London had repeatedly urged restraint, and the high command in Malaya was reluctant to make the move.

Late in the afternoon of December 6, the Supreme Head of the Far East Command, Air Chief Marshal Sir Robert Brooke-Popham, issued orders that included no reference to the *Matador* strategy, but simply brought all forces in Malaya to "the first degree of readiness." At the same time he increased the number of reconnaissance flights over the Gulf of Siam.

The weather the next day was working in Yamashita's favor: squalls and pelting rains severely hampered visibility. Not until evening approached were any sightings made by Brooke-Popham's planes. At 5:30 p.m. some of the Japanese vessels were seen heading toward Singora; at 6:30 others were spotted nearing Pattani, another southern Thai port closer to the Malayan border, and Kota Bharu.

Yamashita's real invasion strategy lay revealed, but his luck continued to hold. Word of the sightings did not reach Far East Command in Singapore until 9:00 p.m.—just three hours before the Japanese transports began to anchor off Singora, Pattani and Kota Bharu.

Nothing seemed to go right for the British from the start.

Royal Air Force planes were dispatched to the Singora area to attack the transports. They scored direct hits on three of the vessels, setting two aflame and causing a third to sink. But the attack had no effect on the invasion. By the time the planes arrived, most of the 5,300 Japanese troops had already debarked.

Brooke-Popham delayed his decision about putting *Matador* into effect until it was too late. And even then, he settled upon a half-measure, sending a battalion of infantry to seize a commanding ridge 30 miles inside Thailand, on the road to Pattani. The battalion was late in starting, was held up at the frontier by Thai constabulary, and was driven out of Thailand by the Japanese before reaching the ridge. Pattani fell without a fight; at Singora, the Thai troops put up a token resistance.

Kota Bharu and its air base proved to be a tougher nut to crack. As the invaders swarmed ashore, they were pinned down by a withering British machine-gun fire from pillboxes behind the beaches. But then one man dashed forward and flung himself across the slit of a pillbox. His comrades charged the blinded position with hand grenades and bayonets, and gradually the coastal defenses were breached. The fields leading to the air base were sown with mines; but the Japanese soldier, schooled to regard suicide as both an honor and a duty, did not hesitate to detonate a mine with his body so that others who followed could cross in safety. In the afternoon, long-range Japanese planes flying in from Indochina repeatedly bombed and machine-gunned the base. At about 4 p.m. its defenders panicked when a false rumor reported enemy ground troops at the perimeter. A pell-mell evacuation began. The station staff set fire to the buildings, the operations room and most of the stores. In their haste, they forgot about the remaining stocks of bombs and fuel and left the runways in usable condition. Within 24 hours of the landings, Kota Bharu and the air base were in Japanese hands.

Yamashita was off to an auspicious start, and he was supremely confident of success in the campaign now under way. For the conquest of Malaya, he would have only 60,000 troops at his disposal, as opposed to 88,000 British. But the numerical superiority did not accurately reflect actual military strength. The British Army in Malaya was a hastily assembled motley of Australian, British, Indian and native Malayan recruits. As already demonstrated at the air base at Kota Bharu, some of the troops were undependable. The two Indian divisions assigned to the defense of northern Malaya lacked leadership; many of their junior officers and noncoms had been pulled out and sent back to India to train new units of raw recruits.

The British Army in Malaya was desperately short of tanks, artillery, communications equipment, even the tools and spare parts needed to repair the machines on hand. Absorbed in other theaters of war, London had given low priority to Malaya's requests for matériel. Moreover, the Army's tactical theories were based on the European model; the available arms and equipment were ill-adapted for the humid tropics, and few of the soldiers were trained or conditioned for jungle fighting—or suitably equipped for it. As one critic noted, they were laden "like Christmas trees," weighed down with packs, haversacks, blankets, gas masks and rations that consisted chiefly of bulky canned goods.

In striking contrast with his British counterpart, the Japanese soldier on the move could manage on a few handfuls of rice and some pickles and preserved seaweed to flavor it. His clothing and weapons were lightweight. And he was no novice in the jungle: the invasion troops had been rehearsed on similar terrain in Hainan and Indochina. Even more important, many of the Japanese troops were experienced in combat, having fought previously in China.

The strategy for the campaign in Malaya was quite simple. From Singora and Pattani, Japanese troops would strike westward across the Kra Isthmus—less than 100 miles wide at that point—then move southward into Malaya and down its west coast, thus bypassing the mountain range in the center of the peninsula. Coincident with the thrust down the west coast, where Malaya's best roads had been built, a secondary drive would be made from Kota Bharu down the east coast. Near the tip of the peninsula, the two forces would converge for an assault on Singapore, the proudest British bastion in the Far East and the main objective of the Malaya campaign.

Residents of Singapore got a taste of what lay in store for them even before Kota Bharu fell. At 4:30 a.m. on December 8, while the invaders were still swarming ashore up north, 17 Japanese Navy bombers roared in to attack Singa-

pore's airfields. Part of their load fell on the congested center of Singapore Town. The city habitually kept late hours, and near dawn still blazed with light. The toll was heavy: some 200 people, mostly Chinese merchants and Sikh night watchmen, were killed or injured, and numerous buildings were destroyed.

An English businesswoman living in a flat above her shop watched incredulously from her window as a blast flattened a store down the road. She telephoned the police. "There's an air raid going on!" she shouted. "Why doesn't somebody put out the lights?"

"Don't be alarmed," she was told. "It's only a practice."

"Well, tell them they're overdoing it!" she snapped.

Singapore was totally unprepared for the raid. Its anti-aircraft gunners were so inexperienced that the British decided not to send up their night fighters for fear that they would be shot down by the city's defenders. Civilian defense offices were not even manned. Only after the bombers had gone were sirens sounded and a blackout considered. But the keeper of the keys to the city's master switches could not be located, and the street lamps blazed on.

The British residents of Singapore concluded that the bombing was a fluke. A time-worn phrase was trotted out: Singapore was—and would remain—an "impregnable fortress," as strong as Gibraltar.

Life as a privileged elite in a lush tropical setting had lulled colonial Britons into complacency. That Japan could pose a serious threat to more than a century of white rule seemed preposterous. In Singapore's whites-only clubs, certain myths had been accepted as gospel. Japanese ships and planes were inferior to those of the West. Japan's small-caliber weapons couldn't even kill a man. The fact that Japanese forces were now bogged down in China was proof not of Chinese resistance but of Japanese ineptitude. The Japanese soldier could neither shoot straight nor fly right because his vision was poor—a result, it was explained, of the same epicanthic fold that gave Japanese eyes their slanted appearance.

Three days after Singapore's baptism of fire, the myths of Japanese inferiority were laid to permanent rest by one of the war's most astonishing episodes. At sunset on December 8, a flotilla of British warships pulled out of Singapore's huge naval base and headed north on a hastily improvised mission: to seek out and sink the Japanese invasion fleet off the Kra Isthmus, and thus—it was hoped—stop the assault on Malaya in its tracks.

Four of the six ships of the task force were destroyers, looking much like pygmies in the company of a pair of giants: the 32,000-ton battle cruiser *Repulse* and the 35,000-ton battleship *Prince of Wales*. Both capital ships were newcomers to Singapore—recently dispatched by London, as East-West tensions heightened, to demonstrate to Japan that however deeply Britain might be enmeshed in war in Europe and North Africa, the British Navy continued to rule the world's seas.

The *Repulse* was a veteran, built in 1915 and since then rebuilt so extensively that wags called her H.M.S. *Repair*. The *Prince of Wales* was spanking new, the Navy's pride and joy; Prime Minister Churchill had chosen her to speed him across the ocean to the Atlantic Charter meeting with President Roosevelt in August.

Aboard the *Prince of Wales,* as the task force moved out of Singapore, was the new commander-in-chief of Britain's Far Eastern Fleet, Admiral Sir Tom Phillips. At five feet four inches, Phillips was inevitably known as "Tom Thumb"—and, alternatively, as "all brains and no body." He had spent 38 of his 53 years in the Navy, and scoffed at the rising

conviction in some quarters that sea power was no match for air power. But if Phillips was feisty, he was also prudent. In outlining his attack plan to his colleagues in Singapore, he had linked its success to two conditions. Catching the Japanese by surprise was essential. And as he neared Singora, where most of Japan's ships were concentrated, he would need fighter cover.

The task force had already sailed when word of developing disaster reached Singapore: the enemy had not only taken Kota Bharu, but had also knocked out all the other airfields in northern Malaya. About five hours out to sea, Phillips received a message from his chief of staff: "Fighter protection on Wednesday tenth will not, repeat not, be possible." The admiral shrugged. "Well," he said, "we must go on without it."

His hopes for secrecy were also doomed. For most of the next day heavy clouds provided a shield against roving enemy aircraft. But in the late afternoon the clouds broke and revealed three planes in the distance, too far off to be shot down. Phillips concluded that his mission was imperiled and, as night fell, the task force turned back for Singapore. But its presence was already known to the Japanese naval command—not from the planes but from a Japanese submarine that had trailed the ships earlier that day.

En route southward, Phillips received another message from his chief of staff, reporting an enemy landing at the port of Kuantan, halfway between the Kra Isthmus and Singapore. The task force might yet serve a purpose; Phillips made for Kuantan. At eight the next morning—December 10—one of the destroyers was sent into the harbor. "All's as quiet as a wet Sunday afternoon," it signaled back.

The reported invaders, later inquiry was to reveal, had been a few water buffalo that had wandered into a field planted with mines as a precautionary measure. Hearing the charges go off, the Indian garrison at Kuantan had assumed the worst and had so informed Singapore.

The task force had been fatefully delayed on its homeward journey. At 10:20 a.m., southeast of Kuantan, a shadowing aircraft was sighted; battle stations were manned. The crews did not have long to wait. At 11 a.m., nine Japanese Navy bombers appeared.

As the *Repulse* and the *Prince of Wales* began taking evasive action, their guns opened fire, sending up a barrage

Japan's conquest of Malaya was launched December 8, 1941, when Lieut. General Tomoyuki Yamashita's 25th Army landed at Singora, Pattani, and Kota Bharu, near the border between Malaya and Thailand. (Thailand was called Siam until 1939, when the name was changed. It switched back to Siam in 1945 and again to Thailand in 1949.) Yamashita's troops advanced west to cut off Malaya at the Kra Isthmus, then swept south along both coasts to Johore, where the British made a desperate stand before withdrawing to Singapore. The island fortress fell 70 days after the campaign began, a month earlier than Yamashita had predicted.

so dense that the spray caused by the falling shells looked to one Japanese pilot like "sand being hurled all over the surface of the sea." But the planes came on, keeping formation, concentrating on the *Repulse*. One bomb hit her amidships and two others grazed her sides, setting several fires. Cecil Brown, an American radio correspondent aboard the *Repulse,* heard a gunner remark grudgingly: "Bloody good bombing for those blokes."

Next came nine low-flying torpedo planes. By zigzagging, the *Repulse* escaped being hit; but a quarter of a mile away, the *Prince of Wales* was struck simultaneously by two torpedoes. Both port propeller shafts stopped and the steering gear failed. A message was flashed to the *Repulse:* "Not under control."

As the *Prince of Wales* began listing, the *Repulse* drew near to see if she could be of any assistance. While the ships were in close, nine more torpedo planes appeared. Three torpedoes hit the *Prince of Wales,* and five struck the *Repulse*. One of them jammed the cruiser's rudder, and she, too, went out of control.

Captain William Tennant ordered all hands on deck and lifeboats lowered. "Good luck and God be with you," he said. The men began scrambling over the side; several of Tennant's officers seized the captain and forced him to come along. At 12:33 p.m. the *Repulse,* listing at about 70°, rolled over and slid into the sea.

New waves of enemy bombers now swarmed around the *Prince of Wales* as she spewed smoke and wallowed in a widening slick of oil. At 1:15 the last bomb hit. The great ship shuddered as if struck by a giant sledge. On the bridge, Admiral Phillips and the skipper of the *Prince of Wales,* Captain John Leach, stood side by side, ramrod straight. They were still there when, five minutes later, the *Prince of Wales* heeled over and sank.

She had just gone under when 11 Royal Air Force fighters appeared, dispatched in response to the only message for help that had come through from the task force. The pilots circled over the scene in disbelief. Hundreds of grimy, exhausted men were clinging to bits of wreckage or paddling about in the sea of oil, giving the thumbs-up signal to the planes overhead—"as if they were holiday-makers at Brighton," one pilot reported—while they were waiting to be picked up by the destroyers of the task force. In all, 2,081

men were rescued, 820 lost. Out of a total of 88 attacking planes, only four were shot down.

It was morning in London when the Admiralty received the news. The Prime Minister was still abed when First Sea Lord Sir Dudley Pound telephoned. In a stricken voice, he conveyed the tidings from Kuantan. "I was thankful to be alone," Churchill later recalled. "In all the war I never received a more direct shock. As I turned over and twisted in bed the full horror of the news sank in upon me. Over all this vast expanse of waters Japan was supreme, and we everywhere were weak and naked."

By the war's fourth day, Japanese bombers had succeeded not only in sinking the *Repulse* and the *Prince of Wales,* but also in crippling British air strength in Malaya. The way was now clear for an all-out drive down the peninsula.

Yamashita had estimated that he could capture Singapore in 100 days. It took 70 days.

Malaya's rugged, jungle-clad terrain seemed made to order for the Japanese. They used their tanks and infantry with great effectiveness on the limited road network. When they came upon a British position, the tanks would rush it, followed by infantry in trucks. If the tanks were stopped, the infantry would attack the position. Approaching a roadblock, the Japanese foot soldiers would melt off the road into the jungle undergrowth or mangrove swamps alongside. In small groups they would move out around the enemy's flanks, padding along the narrow tracks used by native game hunters in the jungle, or poling down the sluggish swamp waterways on crude rafts. Coming up behind the enemy position, they would set up a cacophony of fireworks and other noisemakers, convincing the defenders that they were surrounded by superior forces. The tanks would then take advantage of the resulting confusion by attacking the bewildered troops, sometimes catching British reinforcements in marching columns on the road and wreaking havoc among them.

In these and other situations the simple bicycle proved an invaluable aid to Yamashita's troops. When the tanks were moving up, bicyclists frequently preceded them to reconnoiter the roads ahead. Then, when the enemy had been routed, they would pedal furiously, outpacing their tanks to keep up the pressure on retreating units. Often they served as a mobile force to scout new terrain, fording unbridged streams with bicycles held overhead. Conveniently, Malaya had been a good customer for Japan's bicycles; if a soldier's bicycle needed repair, interchangeable parts were usually available in the next village or town.

The British soldiers were frequently forced to take to the jungle to escape the onrushing Japanese. And of all the harassments they had to endure, it was the jungle that they feared most. They could not bear the sweltering heat, or the bloodsucking leeches or the thorny vines. The tangle of growth frequently limited their visibility to a few feet; there were no natural fields of fire for them to employ when attacking soldiers approached.

The jungle's eerie, pervading stillness also took a psychological toll. A British colonel who visited an Indian unit reported: "They were thoroughly depressed . . . the deadly ground silence emphasized by the blanketing effect of the jungle was getting on the men's nerves."

By the middle of January, Yamashita controlled two thirds of the peninsula. Britain's deteriorating situation spurred a flying visit by General Sir Archibald Wavell, supreme head of the joint American-British-Dutch-Australian command in the Far East. The ground commander in Malaya, Lieut. General A. E. Percival, wanted to continue fighting a delaying action down the peninsula to allow time for reinforcements to reach Singapore. But Wavell ordered a withdrawal all the way to Johore, Malaya's southernmost state, which was separated from Singapore by a shallow channel averaging less than a mile wide.

The fighting in Johore raged for two weeks, and at first seemed to favor the defenders. Yamashita's supply line, always tenuous, by now was stretched almost to the breaking point. The Japanese were running short of ammunition and rations; many of the troops were footsore and sick. Against them were ranged the fresh troops of the 8th Australian Division, which had been held in reserve in Johore. Abandoning static defense tactics, the Australians gave the Japanese a dose of their own medicine, setting ambushes and infiltrating their lines.

Together with Indian troops pulled back from the north, the Australians fought a savage battle in the jungle around the Muar River against Japan's toughest soldiers, the crack Imperial Guards. The British hurriedly sent in 51 Hurricane fighters from England, to try to stop the attackers at the

A BRUTAL MANUAL FOR THE INVADERS

As Japan's invasion fleet got under way for Southeast Asia, every soldier aboard was given a pamphlet marked "confidential" to study. Its author was Colonel Masanobu Tsuji, chief of the invading army's planning staff, and its purposes were to arouse the fighting man to a fever pitch and to enlighten him on a wide variety of subjects ranging from the cultural quirks of the inhabitants to the care of the soldier's health and weapons in tropical conditions. Tsuji, one of his country's more flamboyant military figures, thought so well of his combined ideological tract and how-to manual that he titled it "Read This Alone—And The War Can Be Won." Some excerpts:

In the Japan of recent years we have unthinkingly come to accept Europeans as superior and to despise the Chinese and the peoples of the South. This is like spitting into our own eyes.

Once you set foot on the enemy's territories you will see for yourselves just what this oppression by the white man means. Imposing, splendid buildings look down from the summits of mountains or hills onto the tiny thatched huts of the natives. Money that is squeezed from the blood of Asians maintains these small white mi-

Colonel Masanobu Tsuji, the manual's author

norities in their luxurious mode of life.

After centuries of subjection to Europe, these natives have arrived at a point of almost complete emasculation. We may wish to make men of them again quickly, but we should not expect too much.

Weapons are living things and rifles, like soldiers, dislike the heat. When soldiers rest they ought to give their rifles a rest too, offering them, in place of water, large drinks of oil.

Beware of poisonous snakes. These lurk in thick grass or lie along the branches of trees, and if you do not watch where you put your feet or hands you may well be bitten. If you discover a dangerous snake, you must of course kill it. You should also swallow its liver raw, and cook the meat. There is no better medicine for strengthening the body.

Pineapples and coconuts are good for quenching the thirst, and in mountainous areas you will find that lopping a branch of wisteria and sucking at the open end will prove helpful.

When you encounter the enemy after landing, think of yourself as an avenger come at last face to face with his father's murderer. Here is the man whose death will lighten your heart of its burden of brooding anger. If you fail to destroy him utterly you can never rest at peace.

Before going into the battle area—in the ship at the very latest—you should write your will, enclosing with it a lock of hair and a piece of fingernail, so that you are prepared for death at any time or place. It is only prudent that a soldier should settle his personal affairs in advance.

Muar, but the lumbering Hurricanes proved no match for the faster, more maneuverable Zeroes. Compelled at last to revert to a static front along which they were too widely dispersed, the 4,500 defenders in the Muar area held out for two weeks, but were chewed up piecemeal by the enemy's superior numbers. Still, 900 escaped to safety. The Imperial Guards, counting on totally annihilating the enemy, felt they had lost face. In reprisal, they systematically decapitated 200 wounded Australians and Indians who had been left behind because their comrades were unable to carry them through the jungle.

Finally, the Japanese breached one end of the 90-mile front that had been formed across Johore, exposing the British forces to the threat of encirclement. Orders came to withdraw, and the defenders began their weary exodus to Singapore. But before they pulled back, the Australians gained a measure of satisfaction by catching two companies of Japanese infantry in compact formation and killing most of them from concealed positions.

On the morning of January 31, the remnants of the last British battalion on the mainland—90 very grimy Argyll and Sutherland Highlanders—came over on the 1,100-yard causeway that linked Johore with the island bastion. Two pipers skirling "Hielan' Laddie" played them across. When the last man had crossed over, demolition charges planted by British engineers were exploded, and the waters of Johore Strait poured through a 60-yard gap in the causeway.

Singapore was now isolated and in a state of siege, a smoldering symbol of a dying empire. On the northeast corner the great naval base, which had taken 15 years and millions to build, lay silent and empty beneath the smoke of two huge fires, set by the British even before their troops crossed the causeway. On the island's south shore, the once-bustling waterfront of Singapore Town reeked with the smell of burning rubber; supplies were being destroyed in order to deny them to the enemy.

The Japanese took a week to prepare the assault. Thanks to compatriots who owned some of Johore's rubber estates, good roads had been cut to the very shore of the strait. Over them came masses of matériel, including the big guns that were to shell Singapore and the 200 collapsible boats that were to ferry the troops across.

At 11 p.m. on February 8, the sound of a violent thunderstorm over Singapore was muffled by 440 Japanese guns opening up en masse. The hard-driving Yamashita, who had kept up a relentless pressure on the British all through the campaign, was using up the last of his ammunition as if his supplies were inexhaustible. Under cover of the artillery bombardment, the first wave of Japanese troops embarked for the mangrove swamps on Singapore's northwest shore. A long night of terror ensued for the men who faced the brunt of the assault—two hastily assembled Australian battalions that had just arrived from their homeland and had no combat experience. The Japanese used the same slashing tactics that had won them the mainland, slicing through the defenders and attacking their flanks. Death came at the Australians from all directions. Unfamiliar with the mangrove labyrinth, units separated, got lost.

At dawn, a gunner-signaler at Tengah Airfield, north of Singapore Town, watched some of the survivors in flight.

Marching to the surrender of Singapore, Lieut. General A. E. Percival (far right) the British ground commander in Malaya, is accompanied by his aides, one of them bearing the Union Jack, and another (far left) carrying a white flag. The Japanese officer at center escorted them to the Ford Motor Company's assembly plant on the outskirts of Singapore Town. There, at a bare wooden table, Percival yielded Britain's proud bastion of the Orient to Lieut. General Tomoyuki Yamashita.

"They came moving at a half-trot, panic-stricken," he said. "Most of them were clad only in shorts. Few were wearing boots and most of the men's feet were cut to ribbons. They'd thrown aside their rifles and ammunition. They were panting incoherent, a rabble."

By noon, some 23,000 Japanese troops were moving toward Bukit Timah, a 600-foot hill that dominated the island. A British counterattack failed when communications again broke down. During the following four days, Japanese soldiers repaired the causeway across Johore Strait and brought over their tanks.

Singapore Town was a ruin, subjected to round-the-clock bombing. The streets were a tangle of downed electric wires, splintered telephone poles and overturned cars and trams. Bloated, unclaimed bodies putrefied in a heat made more intense by spreading fires.

More than a million people were herded into an area of three square miles, where half that number had lived in peacetime. The island's water supply was fast running out: of every six gallons pumped into the city's reservoirs, five of them poured out through smashed conduits and pipes. Army deserters—drunk, armed and increasingly belligerent—looted the wrecked shops, stuffing their shirt fronts with cigarettes and food to prepare themselves against the impending collapse of the city.

Even more terrifying was the report of an incident at the military hospital at Alexandra. Japanese soldiers had broken in and run amuck, bayoneting patients and staff alike, killing more than 300 people. Some witnesses had escaped; their stories added to the growing sense of panic.

On Friday morning, the 13th of February, a Japanese plane dropped a note from General Yamashita on General Percival's headquarters at Fort Canning. It was couched in elaborately courteous terms, with compliments for British gallantry and "warriorship"—and a demand for surrender.

Percival cabled the contents to General Wavell in Java, noting that he did not intend to dignify Yamashita's message with a reply. But on Sunday, the 15th, after further advances by the Japanese troops, a conference took place in the bombproof briefing room under Fort Canning. With Percival and his aides was the Australian commander, Major General Henry Gordon Bennett. Fortress Singapore's situation was assayed and found to be hopeless. "Silently and sadly," Bennett recalled, "we decided to surrender."

That afternoon Percival met with Yamashita across a bare table at the Ford Motor Company's bomb-damaged assembly plant on the slope of Bukit Timah. The colloquy was brief. Percival asked for an overnight delay—presumably to have the surrender approved by his superiors abroad. Yamashita, burly and poker-faced, replied that the fighting would go on unless Percival gave his immediate consent. Percival hesitated. "Yes or no?" Yamashita asked. Percival bowed his head and whispered his assent.

At 8:30 p.m. the guns fell silent. The Japanese soldiers began singing "Kimigayo," Japan's slow, stately national anthem. At his headquarters, Yamashita assembled his staff and held the traditional victory celebration of dried cuttlefish, chestnuts and sake. Silently lifting the cups of wine in a solemn toast, the officers faced northeast toward Tokyo.

Yamashita—ever after to be known as the Tiger of Ma-

laya—had achieved a stunning triumph. During the campaign, the British had suffered 138,708 casualties, compared with only 9,824 for the Japanese. In taking the once-proud bastion of Singapore, Japan had dealt a lethal blow to British prestige. Meanwhile, in the early stages of the Malaya campaign, the British in the Far East had suffered another deep humiliation. Japanese forces in superior numbers had crossed over from the Chinese mainland to overwhelm the British garrison at Hong Kong, forcing the surrender of the crown colony on Christmas Day, 1941. With the fall of Singapore, both of Britain's bright jewels in the Orient were gone.

The capture of Singapore gave Japan absolute control of the Malay Peninsula, with its abundant resources of tin, iron, gold, bauxite and rubber. Moreover, it brought the war all the way down to the Strait of Malacca, only 65 miles from Sumatra, the second largest of the Dutch East Indies and the site of some of the richest oil fields in Asia.

The conquest of the Dutch East Indies was already under way when Singapore fell. The Japanese had devised a three-pronged strategy for the capture of the great archipelago. In the east, they planned to move down into the islands of Amboina and Timor, thereby cutting off communications and reinforcements from Australia. In the center, Borneo and Celebes would be seized, and at the far western end of the archipelago, Sumatra would be attacked as soon as Singapore's fall was assured. Finally, when all of these objectives had been taken, the forces involved would be combined for an assault on the island of Java, another major world source of oil and minerals, the center of Allied naval operations in southeastern Asia, and headquarters of the joint Allied military command.

By the time Singapore fell, the Japanese were methodically advancing down through the Dutch Indies, according to plan. Amboina had been captured and Timor was within easy striking distance. Borneo and Celebes had been invaded and the fall of both of those islands was imminent.

On February 14, the day before Singapore surrendered, the first invaders arrived in southern Sumatra as 700 paratroops floated down from the sky over Palembang. The people of that city were already busily destroying the fruits of years of labor and fortunes in investment—the oil fields,

storage tanks and huge refineries of Dutch Shell, and the only supply of high-test aviation gasoline anywhere in the Dutch East Indies. Many of the paratroops were slaughtered, but the fighting halted the demolition work, and before it could be resumed a massive attack came by sea.

Six Japanese cruisers, an aircraft carrier, 11 destroyers and eight transports anchored off the mouth of the Musi River, 50 miles from Palembang. A full infantry division in small craft set out upriver toward the city. In desperation, the outnumbered and outgunned defenders loosed a torrent of oil on the river and ignited it. The flaming cascade incinerated hundreds of Japanese troops, but the weight of numbers prevailed. The Japanese took Palembang the next day—and with it half the oil reserves of the Indies.

Months would be required to restore the oil installations, but meanwhile the Japanese could turn to the final objective in the Dutch East Indies, the neighboring island of Java. The climactic battle for Java began at sea on February 27, when the Allies tried to stop an invasion fleet approaching the island. For the Allies the battle was preceded in the late afternoon of the previous day by a briefing by Rear Admiral Karel Doorman of the Dutch Navy, who commanded the combined Allied naval force. At his headquarters in the leafy old residential quarter of Surabaya, near the Allied naval base, the atmosphere was convivial. The officers were in their starched whites and gold braid. They did not dwell on the daily poundings Japanese bombers were inflicting on Surabaya; instead, they drank toasts to friendships and bet-

With their bayonets flashing, troops of Lieut. General Shojiro Iida's 15th Army present arms in a mass salute shortly before crossing the border between Thailand and Burma. Four months later Burma fell, completing a six-month sweep of Southeast Asia that put more than one million square miles and 150 million people under Tokyo's rule.

ter fortune, and watched a glorious tropical sunset beyond the harbor palms.

The room fell silent as Doorman spoke. Their mission, he said, was to prevent the invasion of Java—to seek out and destroy the enemy convoy now en route. Over charts, he explained his plan and read out the Allies' order of battle. The session was brief and, as some later remembered, the admiral was more than usually charming. As he thanked them and took his leave, the officers saluted. It was the last time they would be together.

That evening, the Allied ships glided through Surabaya's minefield and formed up in open water. Three British destroyers abreast provided a screen up front. Following in line were five cruisers: two Dutch, one British, one Australian, and one American—the U.S.S. *Houston*, which had been reported sunk so many times that her crew had nicknamed her the Galloping Ghost of the Java Coast. Two Dutch destroyers rode the flanks, and four U.S. destroyers brought up the rear.

Doorman's ships were battered from previous engagements, and the crews were exhausted. The combined strike force had no common signal code, no air support, no reliable information concerning the enemy, and—in a region overflowing with oil—a dwindling supply of fuel.

The battle of the Java Sea was joined the next afternoon about 90 miles north of Surabaya, when the Allied ships encountered not one but two Japanese convoys protected by a covering force of three cruisers and 14 destroyers, under Admiral Takeo Takagi. Two of Admiral Takagi's cruisers hove up out of the east, swung all 20 of their 8-inch guns around and let go at extreme range—28,000 yards. "Sheets of copper-colored flame lick along their battle line," U.S. Navy Commander Walter Winslow, aboard the *Houston*, noted in his diary. "My heart pounds wildly as I realize that the first salvo is on the way." The Allied ships roared back, and one Japanese cruiser turned out of the battle line, a fire forward of her bridge.

But Takagi's gunners gave more than they received. One shell screamed into the British cruiser *Exeter* and exploded in the engine room, killing 14 men and knocking six of the ship's eight boilers out of action. The *Exeter*, too, turned out of the battle line. A torpedo slammed into the Dutch destroyer *Kortenser*; the ship folded in two and vanished beneath the water. Three Japanese destroyers appeared; the British destroyer *Electra* took a hail of shells and sank.

At nightfall, Takagi broke contact in order to escort his transports into less dangerous waters. Doorman, aboard the cruiser *DeRuyter*, set off in search of the elusive transports. His force was now reduced to four cruisers, and without air reconnaissance he was groping in the dark.

As Doorman's ships pressed on, Japanese search planes marked their course with smudge-pot flares that burned on the water like jack-o'-lanterns. Under cover of darkness, enemy cruisers closed in on the Allied ships. Around midnight, when the two forces were less than 10,000 yards apart, Japanese gunners fitted 12 new superpowered torpedoes into their tubes and fired.

A tremendous explosion rent the Dutch cruiser *Java*; she plunged, flaming, to the bottom. Seconds later an explosion rocked the *DeRuyter* and a pillar of fire roared into the sky. From the bridge, Doorman ordered the two remaining cruisers, the *Houston* and the Australian *Perth*, to run for home. Then, with one last convulsive blast, the Dutch flagship went down, taking Doorman and 366 of his men.

On February 28, the *Houston* and the *Perth* tried to run the Sunda Strait, between Java and Sumatra, in the hope of escaping into the Indian Ocean. A single reconnaissance plane might have warned them that the Japanese had sealed that passage and were now putting troops ashore near Batavia, Java's capital (later called Djakarta).

While rounding a headland west of Batavia, the *Houston* and the *Perth* suddenly came upon the transports, lying unattended offshore. The cruisers dashed in and sank two transports at point-blank range. Minutes later, a Japanese covering force of three cruisers and nine destroyers appeared on the scene, and a brief, one-sided exchange ensued. Four torpedoes slammed into the *Perth* and sank her. The *Houston* took a salvo of shellfire, and three torpedoes tore open her hull. As the ship lay over to starboard, Commander Winslow was hurled into the oily sea, where he watched her go down. "It seemed as though a sudden breeze picked up the Stars and Stripes and waved them in one last defiant gesture," he remembered. Then, with a shudder, the Galloping Ghost of the Java Coast was gone.

The Japanese landed in Java the next day. Allied aircraft

attacked their transports and landing craft, but there was little effective opposition on the ground. On March 9, in Batavia, the Dutch formally surrendered the Indies, ending three centuries of domination of the archipelago. The last word from Java was broadcast over a commercial radio station. "We are shutting down now," a voice said. "Goodbye till better times. Long live the Queen!"

In Tokyo, Emperor Hirohito was pleased at the news of the Dutch surrender, but he was also uneasy. "The fruits of war are tumbling into our mouth almost too quickly," he told Marquis Koichi Kido, Lord Keeper of the Privy Seal. Japan's military leaders did not see it that way. Flushed with victory, they had already launched an attack against another enemy stronghold in Southeast Asia—Burma, an isolated, mountainous country that had been a British preserve since the late 19th Century.

The immediate advantage of a victory in Burma would be to remove the threat of a counterattack from the north on Japan's new holdings in Malaya and the Indies. But there would be another great gain as well. In the mountains of upper Burma lay the narrow, winding road that was the only usable highway from Allied territory into China. The Burma Road had been agonizingly hacked out of the mountain ranges so that China's Western allies could send in supplies urgently needed in the struggle against Japan's occupying armies. If Burma could be taken, China might be strangled and subdued, once and for all.

The Burma campaign was launched on the morning of December 23, 1941, when about 60 Japanese bombers appeared over Rangoon, which was Burma's capital and military headquarters, as well as one of the busiest ports on the Indian Ocean.

The raiders blasted the dock area and the airfield and killed more than 2,000 people who had flocked into the streets. Some had come out to cheer; long-simmering anti-British feelings, stoked by an underground Burmese independence movement, had suddenly erupted. Other people had come out simply to watch the spectacle.

Six more days of bombing raids followed, launching a terrified mass exodus that clogged the roads leading north, and hampered defense efforts for weeks. Rangoon's population fell from 400,000 to 150,000. Both the administrative

services and civil defense ceased to function, along with fire and medical services. Law and order, always fragile in Rangoon, broke down completely. Dock workers fled, halting all work, and warehouses with crucial military stores lay open to looters.

Meanwhile, a ground attack was launched by troops of Lieut. General Shojiro Iida's 15th Army, moving in from Thailand. By the third week of January, two divisions had broken through the jungle country in the east to the flat rice fields and rubber plantations around the port of Moulmein. Long known to poetry devotees as the site of Kipling's "old Pagoda," Moulmein had a more practical interest for the invaders: it lay only 90 miles southeast of Rangoon.

Among the Allies a conflict arose as to where to make a stand against the Japanese forces approaching from the east. One plan was favored by Major General John Smyth, whose 17th Indian Division was charged with the responsibility for the defense of southern Burma. Smyth proposed that he concentrate his troops on the west bank of the swift-flowing Sittang River, a strong defensive position with a good network of roads for supplies and reinforcements. Smyth's suggestion, however, was vetoed by General Wavell. From his headquarters in Java, Wavell ordered the fight to be waged "as far forward as possible," in the hope that the Japanese advance could be slowed down, and time gained to bring up reinforcements.

And so on February 14, Smyth took a position behind the more easily fordable Bilin River, 30 miles east of the Sittang. After a week in which his forces took serious casualties, Smyth was compelled to pull back to the Sittang with what remained of his division. The attempt to cross to the defensive position on the river's west bank produced the greatest disaster of the Burma campaign.

The only span across the river was a single-lane railroad trestle. British engineers rigged it for demolition, then laid planks across the tracks for Smyth's trucks to drive over. Before dawn on February 22, the trucks began rolling, headlights out, toward the west bank of the Sittang. Smyth, his staff and part of one thinned-out brigade managed to get across. But at about 4 a.m. a truck on the bridge slipped the planks and lodged between the ties. It could not be budged. All traffic came to a complete halt for two and a half hours. The line east of the bridge—trucks, transport mules and thousands of British and Indian soldiers—backed up for six miles along a narrow jungle road.

Then Japanese troops outflanked the line from the north and charged in, driving a wedge between the backed-up British troops and the bridgehead. Entire companies were wiped out. All semblance of order vanished. A number of units broke and ran; half a brigade got lost in the jungle. By nightfall the troops east of the bridge were cut off.

The bridgehead commander, Brigadier Noel Hugh-Jones, faced a cruel dilemma. If the bridge continued to stand, the Japanese could sweep through his fractured forces, cross to the west bank and march on Rangoon. But if the bridge was blown up, all hope of extricating the troops in the bridgehead would be lost.

Hugh-Jones gave the order to blow the bridge. At 5:30 next morning, one soldier recalled, "there was a series of deafening explosions followed by a blinding flash of light and a blast of red-hot air." The bridge reared up; then its wreckage was swept away in the Sittang's swirling waters.

The survivors on the west bank, including a number who managed to swim across from the other side, jammed into trains and headed toward Rangoon. Of the 8,500 men involved from the beginning of the battle, only about 3,500 had made it through alive.

Rangoon was now in its death throes, under relentless attack by enemy planes. Bombs fell, among other places, on the zoo, smashing open the cages; crocodiles and boa constrictors roamed the streets. A minor British official, unhinged by the events around him, released all the prisoners in the jails, all the inmates of the insane asylum, and all the lepers of the leper colony. Then he committed suicide.

On February 27 the Governor of Burma, Sir Reginald Dorman-Smith, cabled London: "I can see nothing in sight which can save Rangoon." Next night he dined at Government House with his aide and two correspondents just in from London. No Indian attendants in long white coats and scarlet waistcoats stood in waiting; of 110 servants, only the cook, the butler and a kennel-keeper remained. As the city burned around them, Dorman-Smith and his guests consumed a three-course meal—the mutton was excellent—and drank the last few bottles of wine from the cellar. Then they repaired to the billiards room for a final game.

The walls were hung with the portraits of Burma's former governors, and apparently something in their steadfast gaze disturbed the Governor's aide. "Don't you think, sir, we ought to deny them to the Japs?" he asked. He then let fly with a billiard ball, and one portrait crashed to the floor. The other guests joined in; smashed paintings of Britain's past grandeur in Burma littered the floor. "It was a massacre," Dorman-Smith later commented.

The Rangoon garrison hung on a few more days, just long enough to receive a new chief: General Harold Alexander, who had served earlier as the commander of the last British troops to leave the beach at Dunkirk, arrived from Calcutta to replace Smyth. Alexander concluded that he might, with luck, save another British Army, even though he could not possibly save Burma. On March 7, he ordered the demolition of the storage tanks of the Burmah Oil Company, outside Rangoon at Syriam. In 70 minutes, 150 million gallons of oil blew up, burning so furiously that a column of smoke billowed up (by estimates of pilots flying past) to a height of some 23,000 feet.

While the detonations thundered, Alexander ordered his troops to move out and head north.

The task of defending the northern part of the country, including the Burma Road, had fallen initially to the 1st Burma Division. Recruited mainly from the hill tribesmen near the China border, the division was made up of ferocious fighters who were dependably pro-British. But in mid-February, the arrival of a Chinese expeditionary force freed the 1st Burma Division to move south and join in the fighting around Rangoon.

The expeditionary force, which was provided by China's Generalissimo Chiang Kai-shek and led by his Chief of Staff, U.S. Major General Joseph Stilwell, consisted of the 5th and 6th Chinese Armies. But despite the imposing titles, the entire force added up to only 50,000 men. With these reinforcements Alexander and Stilwell tried to establish a defensive line in the Prome-Toungoo area, 150 miles north of Rangoon. The Chinese put up a stubborn defense at Toungoo, but they were driven from the city by a numerically superior force and the defensive position collapsed. A third Chinese Army—the 66th—arrived on the scene, but the Burma campaign had turned into a rout. The dramatic denouement of the Burma campaign was yet to come, but the fate of Burma and of Southeast Asia was already sealed.

NIPPON'S ADAPTABLE ARMY

Japanese infantry in Bataan skirt a menacing barrier of sharpened bamboo stakes, planted along their route of advance by retreating Philippine troops.

INGENIOUS TACTICS IN STRANGE LANDS

The war plunged Japan's soldiers into a bewildering variety of climates and cultures, forcing them to devise new tactics and adapt to strange environments. In northern China in the late 1930s they alternately froze and fried while chasing elusive Chinese armies across rutted roads that were converted by the weather into seas of either dust or mud. Within six months of the attack on Pearl Harbor, they were spread across a vast territory stretching 5,800 miles, from the subarctic Aleutian Islands south to tropical Java. Soldiers sent to the front found themselves lurching across Burma on elephants *(right)*, skiing along the shores of the snowbound Kurile Islands, or heaving artillery through heavy jungles on tropical islands. Often troop destinations were so remote and so secret that men perished on barren or jungle-clad outposts without knowing where they were.

Besides the bombs and bullets, the Emperor's soldiers encountered a host of exotic hazards: fearsome thickets of bamboo spears in Bataan, head-hunters in Borneo and, in most places, malarial mosquitoes, bloodsucking leeches and red ants that bit like bulldogs. Some obstacles yielded swiftly to Japanese ingenuity and determination. Agile infantrymen slipped along dim trails through jungles their enemies considered impassable. They crossed streams on improvised bridges and used existing roads by mounting bicycles to pursue retreating foes. An officer who took part in the headlong drive down the Malay Peninsula later expressed fervent thanks "to Britain's dear money spent on excellent paved roads and to cheap Japanese bicycles."

But there were also times when the invaders outsmarted themselves, as in a Trojan-horse scheme for invading neutral Thailand with busloads of Japanese soldiers dressed in bogus Thai uniforms and accompanied by local dance-hall girls. The plan failed when a jittery Japanese secret agent handling operations on the Thai side of the border burned his code book prematurely and was unable to decipher instructions telling him the time and date of the rendezvous. The masqueraders had to hastily change back into Japanese uniforms and fight their way in after all.

In the Philippines, Japanese soldiers wade across a river with their bicycles on their shoulders, while other cyclists ride across a captured bridge.

Japanese soldiers in Burma ford a shallow, boulder-strewn stream on elephants, which were appropriated to transport the troops across the rugged terrain.

Soldiers and horses strain to pull a Japanese supply cart through the mire in northern China. Roads here were so bad that Japanese officers, to keep their Army moving, used not only horses and men as draft animals but also mules, Mongolian camels and dogs.

Imperial Army engineers reinforce an improvised log bridge for use by assault troops pursuing retreating British forces in Malaya. Such expedients, quickly effected, enabled the outnumbered Japanese to push their way rapidly down the Malay Peninsula, denying enemy forces time to rest and reorganize.

On a sweltering island in the Pacific, Japanese soldiers struggle to heave a massive gun carriage into position. Their instructions for moving such heavy equipment were grimly succinct: "Force your way ahead, even if you have to carry the thing on your shoulders."

Camouflaged in white parkas, Japanese ski troops carry out a patrol in Chishima, one of the Kurile Islands guarding the northern approaches to the Japanese archipelago. Ski troops were picked for skill and stamina from residents of Honshu and Hokkaido, the two northernmost home islands.

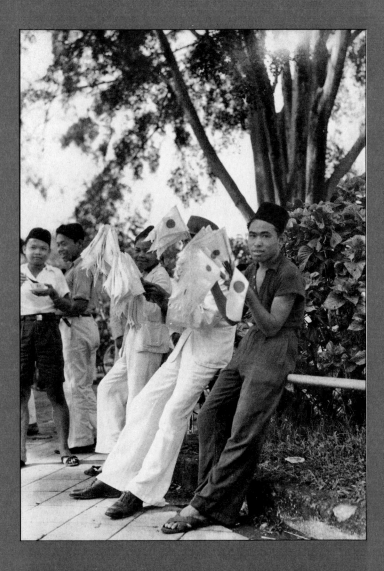

Smiling civilians offer hastily made Japanese flags for sale after the fall, on March 9, 1942, of Bandung, a strategic city in the central Java mountains. In Java, the Japanese received a genuinely warm welcome from the natives, who were happy to be rid of their Dutch masters.

Flag-waving Japanese residents of Bangkok greet victorious Japanese troops entering the city on December 9, 1941. Included among these residents of Thailand's capital were members of Japan's extensive spy network, which had helped prepare the way for the Japanese military machine. The city fell without a fight, and two days later the governments of Thailand and Japan agreed on a treaty of military alliance.

Led by an officer wielding his sword, Japanese soldiers advance through the jungles of New Britain in the South Pacific to storm a blazing native dwelling.

THE FIRST CARRIER CLASH

The target of 93 United States planes, the light carrier Shoho burns and founders in the Coral Sea, marking the first Allied success against a Japanese carrier.

THE BLIND BATTLE OF THE CORAL SEA

The world's first battle between aircraft carriers—and the first major sea engagement between fleets far out of sight of each other—was joined in the spring of 1942 in the Coral Sea. It began on May 4 when a Japanese force shielded by three carriers threatened to occupy the Allied air base at Port Moresby on the southeastern tip of New Guinea. Such an invasion would gain air superiority over the Coral Sea and extend Japanese domination of the South Pacific all the way to the coast of Australia. Hurrying to counterattack came U.S. Task Force 17, including the carriers *Lexington* and *Yorktown*. Steaming in reserve was Task Force 16, built around the carriers *Enterprise* and *Hornet*.

For the first 24 hours, Task Force 17 and the Japanese groped for each other like blindfolded wrestlers, once missing by only 70 miles. Then search planes of both sides found targets. Carrier-based Japanese pilots sank the U.S. destroyer *Sims*, mortally wounded the tanker *Neosho* and mistakenly reported that they had bagged a cruiser and a carrier. The American pilots did better. "Scratch one flattop!" a U.S. squadron leader radioed back to the *Lexington* as the 12,000-ton *Shoho (previous page)* went down.

The next morning both fleets, almost simultaneously, launched their fighters, dive bombers and torpedo planes. The aerial armadas—some 70 Japanese planes versus 83 American aircraft—passed without sighting each other and at 11 a.m. swarmed down on their enemies' empty nests for 45 furious minutes. The box score favored Japan: both of Task Force 17's carriers were hit, the *Lexington* fatally. But in overall effect, the Coral Sea battle was the war's first decisive check to Japan's southward expansion. The Port Moresby invasion was scotched—for good, as it turned out—and the arrival of Task Force 16 *(right)* at the battle's end temporarily thwarted a Japanese plan to extend the invasion to the east by taking the islands of Nauru and Ocean. Moreover, the two big Japanese carriers, the *Shokaku* and the *Zaikaku*, were so badly damaged that they had to limp home for refitting. They were still there, and sorely missed, during the decisive Battle of Midway a month later.

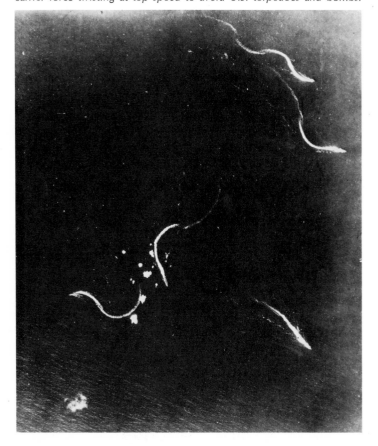

Sinuous white slashes upon the Coral Sea are the wakes of a Japanese carrier force twisting at top speed to avoid U.S. torpedoes and bombs.

Led by the carrier Enterprise (foreground), Task Force 16 secured the American gains in the Coral Sea battle by forestalling invasions of Nauru and Ocean Island.

Wounded but still fighting after Japanese torpedo hits, the U.S.S.
Lexington suddenly erupts from a gasoline vapor explosion (above), setting
off the ship's own torpedoes with a blast that hurls a plane from the
carrier's stern. At right above, a tremendous mushroom cloud billows up
from the carrier; by late afternoon the crew had to abandon ship. At
right below, men climb over the side on knotted ropes while a destroyer
maneuvers through the smoke to take off the wounded. The departure
was as disciplined as a routine drill; some crewmen scooped up the ice
cream remaining in the ship's store, and then neatly lined up their
shoes on deck as if they were expecting to return.

Survivors of the Lexington—many of whom had been with her since her commissioning in 1927—reach out to pull their lifeboat alongside a rescue ship. Though 216 men died as a result of the battle, 2,735 other men and a dog (the captain's cocker spaniel, Wags) went over the side and were rescued without one drowning.

5

In less than six months, the Japanese had seized what the old colonial powers had taken several centuries to acquire. More than a million square miles of land in Southeast Asia—and practically the entire western half of the Pacific Ocean—had come under Japan's domain. More than 150 million people had been added to Emperor Hirohito's subjects. In addition, more than half a million European and American civilians and close to 150,000 military prisoners were in Japanese hands.

The victors were elated—and bewildered. As they soon discovered, holding and exploiting an empire requires even more effort than winning one. By the very size and swiftness of the conquest, Japan had exceeded its capacity to cope with the triumph.

Part of the problem was logistical. The distances between Japan's home islands and the new territories were staggering. A ship setting out from Yokohama for Singapore, for example, had to cover almost as many miles as a ship going from New York to Liverpool. The Japanese Navy failed to recognize the importance of forming its merchant ships into convoys and protecting them adequately in the task of hauling home the newfound riches that were essential to the economy of the nation.

Trouble also loomed in Japan's shortage of trained colonial administrators. Up to now there had been little need for them. The task of managing Manchuria and the occupied areas of China had been left to the military, and the Japanese had assumed that the same type of arrangement would work in other territories they conquered. At a top-secret meeting in Tokyo three weeks before the strike south, the leaders of Japan had decided that until reliable local regimes could be set up, Japanese commanders in the field would exercise absolute authority in the countries that they conquered.

But Tokyo had not expected to win so much so fast. Almost at once, technicians had to be found to staff the banks, businesses, factories, mines and plantations through which Japan could begin to profit from its new holdings. Overseers were needed to supervise native labor; schoolteachers and propaganda specialists, to accustom the myriad inhabitants to new ways of doing things.

A colonial civil service had to be created from scratch. After just a few weeks of contact with Japan's newly in-

UNDER THE CONQUEROR'S RULE

stalled stewards, many of the Southeast Asians who had most joyfully welcomed the lifting of the white man's yoke began to wonder if they had merely exchanged it for another. About the only place where the Japanese tried using politeness was Thailand, which had yielded without a struggle; but the Thais, too, were soon disenchanted. "When our people laugh," one of them observed, "we laugh with all our doors and windows open. The Japanese smile gritting their teeth."

The bureaucrats assigned to administer the newly conquered territories were full of condescension toward the local people and were largely ignorant of their customs and traditions. Grappling with Southeast Asia's diverse cultures, faiths and languages proved to be too much for them. They found it far easier to bully and intimidate than to understand strange ways.

They had only the Japanese military to answer to; the military, in turn, had to answer to no one. The virtually unlimited license Tokyo had granted its field commanders gave them full charge of communications, finance, trade, industry, food and raw materials; they could deal with any recalcitrance they encountered—whether from prisoners of war, foreign nationals, or local populations.

The excesses of which the Japanese military were capable when left to their own devices became clear within days after the fall of Singapore in mid-February of 1942. All of the island's Chinese residents were rounded up and screened, and those who were judged to be anti-Japanese were summarily killed. By Tokyo's own later admission, the victims numbered at least 5,000.

One monstrous aspect of the Chinese Massacres, as they came to be known, was the random nature of the screening process. About the only predictable targets were former employees of the British colonial government and supporters of the Chinese Communists. The fate of some was sealed by hooded local informers who picked them out of "identification parades" as having actively participated in Singapore's defense. Hundreds of others were selected for extinction merely because they bore tattoo marks. In Japan, these markings were a sign that the wearer had a criminal record. They were simply popular adornments among the Chinese but were believed by their captors to signify membership in a secret society.

The executions were supervised by the dreaded *Kempeitai,* Japan's military police. The doomed were shot on the spot, or beheaded, or bayoneted, or taken out of Singapore Harbor in boats and pushed overboard, or driven to beaches and ordered to wade out within convenient range of machine guns set up on the sands at the water's edge.

One of the few survivors, a man named Chua Choon Guan, owed his life entirely to chance. He arrived at a beach in a truck convoy carrying about 400 of his fellow Chinese. They were tied with ropes, lined up in rows, 11 to a row, and led down to the shore. "I was in the fifth row to be machine-gunned," Chua Choon Guan recalled. "They hit me. . . . I fell. . . . The others, who were shot dead, fell on top of me. . . . When I regained consciousness it was dark. I had come to because the tide had come in a little and lapped against my face. I . . . found a sharp rock near the beach and was able to cut the cords by rubbing them against it. I then crawled away and escaped."

The slaughter at Singapore was Japan's way of venting its fury and frustration over the continuing stalemate in its war in China; the overseas Chinese had staunchly supported their homeland's defense. With the surrender of the Dutch East Indies, the Japanese settled another sort of score.

Enraged at finding so many of the coveted oil fields set afire, they took out their wrath on the government officials and oil-company personnel deemed responsible. At Balikpapan, in Dutch Borneo, the entire white population was dispatched; some had their arms and legs lopped off with swords, while others were driven into the sea and shot. A similar fate befell all the white males at Tjepu, in Java; their wives and daughters were spared—then repeatedly raped as the Japanese commander looked on.

It had been assumed that Japan's treatment of military prisoners would be governed by the humanitarian terms of an international treaty on the subject that had been drawn up at Geneva in 1929. Early in 1942, by way of neutral intermediaries, the Allied powers informed Tokyo of their intention to observe the Geneva Convention with the prisoners of war they captured, and they requested that Japan, which was one of the signatories to the pact, reciprocate. In response, Foreign Minister Shigenori Togo pointed out that the Japanese Diet had never ratified the Convention; nevertheless, he added, his country would comply with its terms *mutatis mutandis*—"with the necessary changes."

This simple Latin phrase, a familiar legal usage, gave the Japanese a large loophole, enabling them to flout the Convention at will.

In practice, the Japanese chose to deal with their prisoners according to their own centuries-old code known as *Bushido*—literally translated, "the way of the warrior." It was the deep-rooted Japanese belief in the code that had led them to decide against ratifying the Geneva Convention: the two were contradictory. *Bushido* equated compassion with weakness.

On the basis of this ancient code, the modern Japanese had devised certain rules of behavior for the battlefield. If a retreat from an area became necessary, every hospitalized Japanese soldier understood that he might be shot by the medical officer in charge or given a hand grenade and told to kill himself. The sick and the wounded were "damaged goods"—men who were no longer "complete," and thus were expendable.

Above all, surrender to the foe was forbidden. The Japanese soldier was required to commit suicide instead, else suffer eternal disgrace in the eyes of his country and his family. Such ignominy awaited even the soldier who was taken captive while unconscious as a result of an injury.

Japan's prisoners of war encountered a credo totally alien to them. They had been taken alive; far from feeling disgraced, they were delighted to have survived, and they asked that their names and addresses be sent home so their families could share their relief—a right granted them by the Geneva Convention. To their captors, they merited utter contempt, hence every sort of abuse.

In all, Japan maintained about 300 prisoner-of-war camps throughout its conquered territory and home islands—and there was no consistency in the way they were run. In some of the camps, the prisoners were treated well, at least most of the time, and the discipline was extremely lax. At Zentsuji, Japan, where Guam's defenders ended up, prisoners were issued used Japanese Army clothing and a ration of 30 cigarettes a week. In Bandung, Java, the Dutch prisoners were permitted to open a canteen that served choice steaks smothered with onions. At Changi, on Singapore Island, the guards' supervision was sometimes so casual, especially on Imperial holidays, that enterprising Australians once walked

out of the camp gate, set up a roadside stand and did a land-office business selling passersby gasoline from a hidden supply dump at five dollars a gallon. They made several thousand dollars before they were caught.

At other times—in the same camps and elsewhere—the Japanese were cruel captors. The punishment meted out to the Australian entrepreneurs—two weeks in the blazing sun without washing facilities or latrines—was mild compared to the barbarities inflicted elsewhere for far lesser infractions, or for no reason at all. In Makassar, where a number of survivors of the Battle of the Java Sea were imprisoned, the men were routinely beaten with iron pipes, as many as 200 blows per beating, enough to reduce human flesh to pulp. On the deck of a ship bound for Shanghai, five American prisoners from Wake Island were decapitated without any explanation whatever; they might have been guilty of failing to secure permission to speak, or to walk about, or to climb up the ship's ladders—all punishable by "immediate death," according to the regulations the prisoners were handed before embarking.

Even prisoners not singled out for punishment often suffered miserably. Hundreds of men were jammed into space that had been intended for dozens. They usually slept on mud or bare concrete floors or in bunks without springs.

The Chairman of the Executive Commission

requests the honor of your company

at a Reception

in celebration of the victory of the

Imperial Japanese Army and Navy

in the Philippines

to be held on

Monday, May the eighteenth

nineteen hundred and forty-two

from five to six o'clock in the afternoon

Malacañan Palace

Latrines were makeshift. Medical supplies were doled out grudgingly, if at all.

Starvation rations were standard fare. At Tarlac in the Philippines, where General Wainwright and fellow officers were taken after the fall of Corregidor, the diet consisted chiefly of rice, "with an ounce or two of either pork or beef thrown in once every week or two," Wainwright recalled. The Japanese later contended that Wainwright received the same kind of diet that was fed to their own soldiers. But for Wainwright, the quantity and quality were insufficient. He lost 40 pounds in four months.

Under such conditions, humor offered the only relief. When the Japanese demanded that a group of British prisoners sign a pledge stating that they would not try to escape, each man complied while muttering "I sign under duress." One of them explained to the suspicious officer in charge that it was an old English custom to say a prayer when signing an important document. A young British Army doctor, Captain Stanley Pavillard, devised a form of "occupational therapy" for his fellow inmates. As he later described it: "We devoted much time and effort to the pursuit and capture of bugs and lice, which we then slipped in vast quantities into the Japanese soldiers' huts."

Harder times were in store for Captain Pavillard and his confederates. Toward the summer of 1942, they were told they would be moved north to rest camps in Malaya's mountains; the Japanese administrator assured them that they would get better food and sanitary conditions there. The men were indeed moved north—to the steaming jungles of the Thai-Burmese border, along a river that was known as the Kwai Noi. There they learned what the true purpose of their journey was: together with Japanese railroad construction troops, prisoners from camps in Java and Sumatra and a force of conscripted native laborers, they were to hack out the primeval jungle growth and lay the track for a new railroad that was to link Bangkok and Rangoon (the project was later made the setting for the fictional *Bridge over the River Kwai*).

In a 41-nation pact made at The Hague in 1907, Japan had agreed not to use military prisoners for work that was either excessive or in any way connected with war. The Thai-Burmese railway project was of immense strategic value to the Japanese; increasingly harried by Allied attacks in the sea lanes between Bangkok and Rangoon, they needed an overland link to maintain their supply lines.

The climate, combined with the pressure to complete the railway, created a situation that was intolerable for the prisoners. Ernest Gordon, who had served as a company commander in the Argyll and Sutherland Highlanders, later described his ordeal:

"Every morning as soon as dawn streaked the sky . . . we were marched from Chungkai to work at hacking out the route for the railroad. We were not marched back until late at night. . . . We did this seven days a week. We lost all consciousness of time. Was it Tuesday, the fourth, or Friday, the seventeenth? Who could say? And who cared?

"Except for our G-strings, we worked naked and barefoot in heat which reached one hundred and twenty degrees. Our bodies were stung by gnats and insects, our feet cut and bruised by sharp stones. . . . Somewhere the guards had picked up the word 'Speedo.' They stood over us with their nasty staves of bamboo yelling 'Speedo! Speedo!' until 'Speedo' rang in our ears and haunted our sleep. . . . When we did not move fast enough to suit them—which was most of the time—they beat us."

Some victims of the beating simply "slid to the ground and died," Gordon recalled. Other men died of thirst, hun-

御案内申上候　御素内申上候
昭和十七年五月十四日

比島行政長官

ホルヘ・ビ・バルガス

拝啓陳者來ル九月十八日午后五時ヨリ同
六時迄マラカニヤン・パレスニ於テ比島ニ
於ケル大日本帝國陸海軍ノ戦捷ヲ慶祝ス
ル爲メ祝賀會相催候間御來駕被下度此段

敬具

Invitations to Japan's victory celebration in the Philippines, engraved in English and Japanese, were addressed to members of the islands' ruling body, the Philippine Executive Commission, as well as to leaders of the conquering army. About 300 persons attended the command-performance celebration, which followed a victory parade through Manila's streets and was held at Malacañan Palace, the official residence of the Philippines' chief of government, Jorge B. Vargas.

ger or exhaustion; cholera, dysentery, malaria and tropical ulcers claimed others. The eventual toll came to approximately one third of the 46,000 prisoners employed—and nearly half of the 150,000 native laborers. When the final figures were known, it was estimated that each mile of the 250-mile railway had cost 64 Allied and 240 native lives. Moreover, the Japanese estimated that 1,000 of their own soldiers had also died.

On the whole, the enemy civilians who had been caught in the tide of conquest were spared the naked brutalities visited upon the military prisoners. Theirs was a subtler form of torment: the Japanese simply dumped them behind the guarded gates of internment camps and left them there to fend for themselves.

Tokyo felt no obligation to see to their care and feeding; the mood of the camp administrator determined whatever meager fare was provided, if any. Carl Mydans, a Life photographer who was interned at Manila's old Santo Tomás University, later commented: "I'm not saying that our captors did not feed us well, or even enough. During the first six months, they did not feed us at all." Mydans, his wife and their fellow inmates would have starved if Filipino friends and faithful former servants had not flocked daily to the high, iron picket fence around the campus and thrust food packages through the bars. Internees elsewhere were less lucky: their sustenance depended on the pickings they gleaned from their captors' garbage.

Survival became a matter of individual ingenuity and stamina—a test of one's ability to do without medicine,

bedding, adequate clothing, decent shelter. Santo Tomás, sprawled over 53 acres, was a haven compared to other places the Japanese designated as camps. A Singapore prison that had been built to accommodate 600 housed 2,800 British civilians; in Borneo, 33 women and children, including the author Agnes Newton Keith and her small son, were quartered a mile from a leper colony in a quarantine station that the British government had used for housing incoming Asians. "That leaking, rotting, unventilated, unlighted, wooden-windowed building," Mrs. Keith later wrote, "was retribution on us Europeans for allowing such a place to exist for the housing of anyone."

The hardships were emotional as well as physical. Mydans remembered lying awake "assessing how I felt: defeated, trapped, cut off. All these I might have expected. But more than these I felt the burden that is so heavy on all prisoners: lack of self-respect."

Ironically, the failure of the Japanese to establish any sort of program for life in captivity helped to keep many internees on an even keel. The prisoners were forced to devise their own programs, drawing upon the wide assortment of talents available; among their numbers were teachers, missionaries, businessmen, doctors and engineers. At Palembang Jail in Sumatra, language classes were conducted in Dutch, English, Malay, Spanish, French, German, Russian and Japanese, while a newly formed Palembang Jail Engineering Association held regular symposia on a wide variety of technical subjects.

The Japanese permitted the internees to manage their camp affairs—up to a point. The occupants of Santo Tomás

grew their own vegetables and held contests every week for the cleanest living quarters. They published a newspaper (*Internews*), staged variety shows (the first offering: a tap dancer, two trumpet imitators, an accordion solo) and constructed a sprawling campus shantytown out of bamboo and nipa palms with subdivisions that they called "Frog Bottom" and "'Toonerville."

But even in the most relaxed camps, reminders of the absolute authority of the camp commandant were ever-present. Internees were required to bow to all guards, and were punched or slapped for failure to do so—or to do so properly. And the specter of the *Kempeitai* hovered over all. At any time, on any pretext, these agents turned inmates out of their quarters for searches—discovery of a short-wave radio meant death for the owner—and carried them off for interrogation and torture.

At Manila's Fort Santiago, a maze of dungeons and torture chambers built in the 16th Century for the Spanish Inquisition, more than a dozen targets of investigation were pressed into a 10-by-10-foot cell shared by flying cockroaches. There was no room to lie down. "It was agony to stand hour after hour, day after day," wrote Frederic Stevens, an American who spent seven months in Santiago.

Agony found occasional respite in the loss of consciousness induced by torture. Prisoners were force-fed water, then spread-eagled so their tormentors could jump on their stomachs. Others, hands tied behind them, were hoisted by their wrists until their toes barely touched the floor, then kicked, beaten and left hanging for hours. One day, an incensed interrogator cut a piece of skin from Stevens' hand and made him eat it. "How the other Japanese laughed at this joke!" he reported. At night the prison echoed with other sounds: "The groans of tortured and beaten prisoners . . . the clanging and dragging of leg irons . . . the tears of those who in the night let their emotions go," Stevens wrote, ". . . could not help but bring forth the cry, 'My God, my God, why hast Thou forsaken me?'"

Native Southeast Asians viewed the humiliation of their former colonial masters with mixed emotions. Some gloated; others were appalled. But nearly all shared initially in the feeling that the Japanese victory would spell better times for them.

Shrewd prewar propaganda[...] Tokyo, had created this optimi[...] alist movements that had beg[...] rule, the Japanese had paint[...] for the Asians," in which [...] independent—and thrivin[...] nomically self-sufficient '[...]

Disillusionment came [...] the Japanese banned al[...] and the spreading of "fa[...] the press and forbade listening [...] casts; all radio receivers had to be fixed so [...] be tuned only to Japanese-controlled stations.

A determined effort was made to wipe out all Western influences. Music and movies from America were prohibited. Western languages, an executive order declared, "have ceased to exist"; letters not addressed in Japanese or the native language went undelivered. Schools were closed pending the completion of a new curriculum that included the compulsory study of Japanese and a history of Asia rewritten for Asians. In their thoroughness, the Japanese even replaced the Roman calendar with their own: 1942 became 2602, denoting the number of years since the first Japanese emperor had ascended the throne.

For ordinary Southeast Asians, the Japanese presence became a nuisance, a constant insult, and an ever-looming menace. Under pain of arrest, they had to carry identification cards to be produced at checkpoints throughout cities, special passes for out-of-city travel and—in many places— armbands denoting the degree of trust the Japanese put in the wearer. Infractions of the conquerors' rules invited grilling by the *Kempeitai*, one of whose favored practices— pulling out the victim's fingernails—even became the subject of a wry jest leveled at indiscreet natives by their friends: "Do you need a manicure?"

Like the military prisoners and Western internees, natives had to bow to all Japanese, and were slapped in the face if they failed to do so. Though slapping was a common form of rebuke in the Japanese Army, it was regarded by Southeast Asians as a particularly degrading insult; it especially offended the *machismo* of the Filipinos. As for the bow itself, it was a great humiliation to the Indonesian Muslims: it was supposed to be performed bareheaded, and the

The popular young nationalist leader of the Dutch East Indies, Achmed Sukarno, is decorated by a Japanese officer. Sukarno served as chief advisor and propagandist for the Japanese after they occupied the colony and pressured them to grant his country its independence. When the war was over, he became the first president of the new nation of Indonesia.

...aps as a sign of their faith. The Japanese ... skullcaps off with their rifle butts.

...heralded Co-Prosperity Sphere proved an-... of disenchantment; in the privacy of their ...usinesses, Southeast Asians were soon calling it ...Poverty Sphere." The most lucrative enterprises ...ken over by Japan's biggest companies, the *zaibatsu;* ... was not appropriated by the great mercantile firms ...nt to smaller Japanese traders formed into syndicates.

Native wage earners fared no better than native entrepreneurs. Almost overnight, the war had shut down the Western import-export houses, the great agricultural estates and other sources of employment. With a glut on the labor market, the Japanese cut wages: in the East Indies, the day rate fell to half of what it had been under the Dutch. At the same time, inflation soared. Japan liquidated all enemy banks (including American Express) and replaced them with its own Southern Regions Development Bank, which poured in a torrent of unbacked currency. Filipinos dubbed it "Mickey Mouse" money; they soon had to carry a whole satchelful of it to purchase a single banana.

To cap matters, both consumer goods and food supplies began to run short. Japan was not equipped to provide the wares formerly imported from the Western nations; nor could it spare the shipping to relieve the food scarcities. While surplus rice stores rotted on Rangoon's docks, Filipinos went hungry. In Batavia, the rice warehouses were full, but the food was reserved for the use of the Japanese, and protected by armed guards. When desperate residents of the city stormed the warehouses, the Japanese called out the city's entire populace, beheaded some of the culprits before the assemblage, and displayed the heads on poles as a warning against future raids.

Japan's sole success in its dealings with the Southeast Asians was inadvertent. In the search for native talent to run the pliable regimes now being set up, the budding nationalist movements offered a promising source of supply. But in fostering many of the youthful zealots in these movements, the Japanese unleashed forces beyond their power to control. As it turned out, the conquered countries had to await the resurgent Allies to gain their independence, but the impetus toward that end was provided, however unintentionally, by the Japanese.

Their real purpose was self-serving: every recruit to the cause of collaboration helped tighten Japan's imperial grip. When and if his usefulness ended, the Japanese were prepared to discard him. A fiery young Burmese radical named Aung San was one of the first to learn this lesson. Well before Pearl Harbor, Japanese intelligence agents secretly recruited Aung San and a group of his compatriots known as the Thirty Comrades, trained them in jungle warfare on Hainan Island, then brought them back home with the invading Japanese forces as the nucleus of the Burma Independence Army. They were to recruit their own troops and, so the Japanese promised, were to inherit a free Burma once the British were expelled.

The Thirty Comrades kept their part of the bargain. By the time Rangoon fell, the Burma Independence Army numbered close to 30,000, and was moving out in pursuit of the retreating British. But within a few months, the Japanese disbanded the Burma Independence Army, swept Aung San aside, and enlisted a group of old-line Burmese politicians to front a Japanese occupation government.

Collaborators fared better in the East Indies—for a time. Initially, the Japanese were welcomed there, not only as liberators but also as the fulfillment of an ancient prophecy. According to widely accepted lore, Djojobojo, a Javanese king in the 14th Century, had predicted that his countrymen would suffer three centuries of subjugation under a white race, then would be freed by yellow people from the north. The Japanese were believed to be those people.

The Japanese exploited the situation in every way possible. To win over skeptical Islamic leaders among the predominantly Muslim population, propagandists had begun even before the war to emphasize the similarities between Shinto and Islam. They spoke fervently of the possible conversion of the Emperor to the Prophet Muhammad's faith, and painted a dazzling picture of a future Islamic world empire centering around Japan's Emperor-Caliph. After the Dutch East Indies were conquered, they opened a Religious Affairs Office to gain influence and authority in the Muslim community. At the same time, to ingratiate themselves with the local population, the Japanese lifted the Dutch ban on singing the anthem and flying the red-and-white flag preferred by native patriots.

But the shrewdest move made by the Japanese—so they

thought—was to bring an immensely popular and charismatic young nationalist named Sukarno out of his Dutch-imposed exile to help whip up popular sentiment against the Allies and for the Japanese. To spread their propaganda, the Japanese expanded the archipelago's radio network; they busily installed receivers in every city square, erected "singing towers" at key points throughout the cities, and set up loudspeakers tied into the network in distant villages. Through them all came Sukarno's voice, extolling the Japanese, condemning the Allies—and pouring forth a steady stream of double-talk that soared past Japanese censors but was understood by his compatriots only too well.

Sukarno's main weapon was language, and he employed it well. The Japanese detested the terms "Indonesia" and "Indonesians," which conjured up an undivided nation; they preferred the divisive implications of "natives of Java" and "natives of Sumatra." Sukarno blithely employed the collective usage—and got away with it.

In the Philippines, Japan faced a unique situation. For 40 years the United States had encouraged and developed Filipino participation in the colonial government. During that time, a body of skilled Filipino political and judicial leaders had emerged to staff a full-blown, functioning government, which the Japanese fervently hoped could be won over to their side. But Washington had promised the Filipinos complete independence by 1946, and they saw no reason to rally voluntarily to the enticement of some undated liberation by Japan. The war, as they saw it, was as much their struggle as America's. When the Japanese invaded Bataan in 1942, the Filipino and American forces resisted them as one U.S. Army, and President Quezon demanded his people's unswerving allegiance to the Allied cause.

Less than 72 hours after the Japanese occupied Manila, General Homma's chief of staff began calling on Filipino leaders, urging them to come over to the New Order. In response, some 30 Filipino leaders, including Quezon's executive secretary, Jorge Vargas, Secretary of Justice Jose P. Laurel, an avowed Japanophile, and Congressman Benigno Aquino, whose own son was fighting on Bataan, held a series of meetings to decide on a course of action.

They had no real guidelines. At Quezon's last full Cabinet meeting before he departed for Corregidor, Laurel had begged for direction: how were those left behind to deal with the Japanese without committing treason? Quezon had mentioned something about keeping faith with America, and had also relayed the purported feelings of General MacArthur on the subject. "What can you do under the circumstances?" MacArthur was supposed to have said. "You have to do what they ask you to do, except one thing—the taking of an oath of allegiance to Japan."

MacArthur later denied having said this. But largely on the basis of the alleged guidelines, the Filipino leaders delivered a "letter of response" to Homma on January 23, pledging obedience and cooperation "to the best of our ability." They took this course, they assured themselves, to mitigate their people's suffering under the heel of the invader. Three days later, the new Philippine Executive Commission, made up of these men, became the nucleus of the Japanese puppet government.

Chief Justice Jose Abad Santos defined the alternative. He had accompanied Quezon to Corregidor, but remained in the Philippines when Quezon was evacuated to Australia. In May he was captured by the Japanese and confronted with a demand that he collaborate. Abad Santos flatly refused—and was executed by a Japanese firing squad. His death underscored the schism that now rent the incipient nation. For in choosing to cooperate with the Japanese—however that decision was later explained—the Filipino leaders had broken with the people they professed to lead. Like Abad Santos, the vast majority of Filipinos had chosen to resist.

On May 18, less than two weeks after Abad Santos's execution, the members of the Philippine Executive Commission marched in the Japanese victory parade through Manila, carrying little Japanese flags. Some of the people along the parade route pointedly turned their backs when the color guards passed; most stood mute and impassive as thousands of Japanese soldiers went by in trucks and tanks and on foot, paced by the martial music of Japanese and Filipino bands.

But as the last Filipino band came abreast of the reviewing stand, a great cheer arose from the spectators nearby. In the stand, General Homma and his aides looked surprised and pleased, and smilingly acknowledged the outburst.

The onlookers dispersed, still hugging the secret they shared: the piece the last Filipino band had chosen to play was "The Stars and Stripes Forever."

A NEW ORDER IN ASIA

In the Philippine Islands, where English was a second language for many of the people, a Japanese soldier teaches school children the conquerors' tongue.

AN ABRUPT END TO COLONIAL RULE

When the Japanese conquered Southeast Asia, they were planning to create an empire that they would dominate not only in a military sense, but politically, economically and culturally as well. The way to accomplish this seemed simple enough. First, they would overrun a country and set up military rule or a puppet regime. Then they would eliminate the evidence of European domination, free any political prisoners and remold the population in the Japanese image. The vanquished would be persuaded that they shared a common Asian heritage with their conquerors, and a new Asian economic community, to be known as "The Greater East Asia Co-Prosperity Sphere," would be established with Japan as its center.

But in practice the program was carried out so fast and with so little finesse that it proved a failure. When earnest Japanese cultural missionaries tried to teach the local peoples the Japanese language, and associations were formed to study the ideals of Japanese womanhood, the suspicion grew that one kind of imperialism was being substituted for another. Tired longshoremen and businessmen were antagonized by being forced to spend their spare time listening to long lectures on such subjects as "Nippon History and Things Nippon."

Moreover, it quickly became apparent that the conquerors were more interested in helping their own economy and fueling the Japanese war machine than in forming a cooperative economic venture. The Japanese requisitioned great quantities of foodstuffs, causing shortages in the lands they had overrun. They paid for the requisitioned supplies with forged Indian rupees in Burma and with worthless scrip in Thailand, Malaya and Indonesia. They expropriated raw materials and disrupted traditional agriculture by forcing farmers to grow cotton and other crops needed in Japan. Moreover, they treated their prisoners with such severity and showed such condescension toward the local peoples that by the time the Allies launched their counterattack, they found a number of native-organized resistance groups ready to fight at their side.

Determined to eradicate all traces of colonialism, workmen in Singapore dismantle a statue of Sir Stamford Raffles, the British founder of the city.

A political prisoner in Batavia, Java, jailed under Dutch colonial rule, awaits his release by the Japanese. The city was the capital of the Dutch East Indies.

American civilians, interned at Santo Tomás University on the outskirts of Manila, collect bags of food and other supplies brought to them by friendly Filipinos. For the first six months of their captivity, the 3,500 prisoners at Santo Tomás were issued no food at all by the Japanese, but in an area of the camp that was known as "the fence" they were permitted to accept the necessities of life from their friends.

(NOTICE)

(1) Salute to the Japanese soldiers when you meet them.
(2) The Japanese flag should be displayed at every house's door.
(3) Every body must put the sun-rise arm band on the left arm.
(4) Every body should have the certificate of residence.
(5) Wherever you see Japanese soldiers you must welcome them and not escape from them. The escaper will be considered as the enemy.
(6) Unless you do not tell false prices you will be payed reasonabl[y]
(7) You are absolutely prohibited to walk from the sun-set untill [ ] without carrying lamps. The walker who has not lights will [ ] by the Japanese patrolling soldiers without any warns.
(8) Don't be fooled and bewildered by false propagand[a] munists bandits and chinese.
(9) The incendiarism accidental fire and robbery will be [ ]
(10) The holding of arms is allowed by the army, But the[ ] holder should report to the mayor it and get permission fro[m]
(11) The Jobless people can find one's jobs in Japanese army and [ ]
(12) Be obdient to the orders of governor and mayor who are authorized

(Commander in Chief
Imperial-Japaness force)

Rules and regulations governing the behavior of the Philippine civilian population under the Japanese occupation are posted on a fence outside the Santo Tomás internment camp by order of the conquerors' commander-in-chief. Civilians were required to salute Japanese soldiers, carry lamps after dark, and obey all orders of the occupying authorities.

A battered bathtub propped up on lumber scraps serves prisoners at Santo Tomás as a sink for hair washing. Housed in two university buildings where the plumbing was badly clogged, the prisoners had to improvise bathing and other sanitary facilities.

British POWs, among 61,000 Allied captives forced to help build a rail link between Japanese bases in Thailand and Burma, labor in steaming jungle heat under the eye of a Japanese guard. Lacking mechanical engineering equipment and mercilessly lashed by their overseers, work crews completed the 250-mile railway almost entirely by hand in a little more than a year—but at a staggering cost in lives. The prisoners were half starved, riddled with untreated malaria, dysentery and jungle sores, and driven beyond human endurance; about a fifth of them died.

In order to help make up for a shortage of raw cotton in Japan, closely guarded Filipino villagers are forced to plant cotton in a field that was formerly used to grow sugar cane as a food crop.

Wasted by months of hunger and disease, Dutch prisoners stare
listlessly across the barbed wire of a prisoner-of-war camp in Sumatra. One
Dutch woman who survived the horror of a Sumatran concentration
camp later recalled what shocked her most about her fellow prisoners: "It
was the expression of their eyes. They had what I can only describe as
'dead eyes.' " The conquerors, charging that Japanese residents in the
Dutch East Indies had been brutally rounded up after Pearl Harbor,
were especially harsh with Dutch captives in retaliation.

Women internees at a concentration camp at Singapore, assembled for roll
call, bow before their captors in a ritual required by the Japanese.
Prisoners were made to stand at attention first, then bend at the waist to a
15° angle and remain silent in that position to a count of five.

THE PATRIOTIC ART OF WAR

In this rendering of the invasion of Guam, Kohei Ezaki caught the menacing realism of modern warfare within the delicate tracery of a Japanese seascape.

A SENSE OF BEAUTY IN AWESOME EVENTS

From the outset of World War II, Japan, like Nazi Germany, mobilized its cultural resources to promote the war effort. Artists, writers and composers were urged to join national associations where they were trained to channel their talents into producing patriotic works and making money for the state. No one who failed to support these objectives could hope to have his work published or performed.

But unlike their German counterparts, who quickly became mired in heavy-handed celebrations of Nazi prowess, Japan's painters displayed a sense of beauty and design that lifted much of their work above the level of mere propaganda. Portrayers of fragile plum blossoms and serene landscapes before the war, they managed to retain a delicate, mystic touch as they depicted scenes of fighting men and fiery destruction.

Commissions dispensed by the War Ministry were highly coveted, and the best of the martial art was displayed each year at an immensely popular exhibit sponsored by *Asahi Shimbun,* the largest Tokyo newspaper. Some of the best war paintings produced by Japanese artists are shown on these pages. The painters who created them were well established and worldly-wise when the war began. Many of them had studied in Paris before the war, rubbing elbows with expatriate artists of a dozen nations, and absorbing the techniques of many different styles of painting.

When Japan invaded China in 1937, artists by the hundreds surged to the mainland to portray battlefields where their countrymen had triumphed. Then as the arena of war broadened from the Aleutians all the way to New Guinea, the more venturesome painters followed close behind the advancing troops, sketchpads in hand. Others, who stayed at home, painted battle scenes from military photographs. Often the result was a blending—to today's viewer somewhat incongruous—of Western near-photographic realism with traditional Oriental styles.

Apart from its evident esthetic appeal, the war art fulfilled its immediate function: to help rouse a nation in support of Japan's imperial adventures.

Hong Kong under attack in 1942 was painted by Hoshun Yamaguchi, a famous Japanese artist, from sketches he made there during the Occupation.

A thunderous bombardment of Cavite Navy Yard, near Manila, is portrayed by Chosei Miwa, who was a painter of flowers before the war.

Grimly realistic bombers intrude above a forbidding Aleutian landscape in a painting by Osamu Ogawara. The snow-covered peaks of Attu rise precipitously in a classic Oriental perspective technique that makes the successive ridges stand out sharply. Ogawara worked from photographs taken during the Japanese occupation of the islands in 1942 and 1943. The lines that are visible in the reproduction are probably the result of the painting's having been folded for storage or transport.

Artist Shori Arai sailed with the Japanese Fleet from Rabaul to record these cheerful pastel vignettes of life aboard an aircraft carrier. His paintings reflect the vitality and careful attention to detail of his countrymen's 18th and 19th Century master printmakers. Above, maintenance crewmen repair torpedo bombers on the ship's hangar deck. At right above, a squadron of Zeroes warms up for takeoff; below, a light dive bomber climbs into the wind to the farewells of the flight-deck crew.

The silent descent of paratroops in the 1942 assault on Menado, a Celebes port, was treated in a tranquil, dreamlike style by artist Tetsu Katsuda.

6

To the few people at Pearl Harbor who knew of his function there, Lieut. Commander Joseph Rochefort's foibles were well worth indulging. As his working attire, the chief of the 14th Naval District's Combat Intelligence Unit favored an ancient red smoking jacket and carpet slippers. His usual working day was a 20-hour stretch polished off by a nap on his office cot. The office, a windowless basement room behind a steel door, was hardly a showcase of Navy spit and polish; desks, chairs and floor were awash in papers.

But there was no doubt about Joe Rochefort's brilliant gift for cryptanalysis. In 1940 he had helped crack JN-25, the Japanese Navy's operational code. It was his report of Japan's intention to seize Port Moresby that had sent Task Force 17 into battle in the Coral Sea.

Now, in mid-May of 1942, Rochefort was convinced another major enemy move was coming. The air crackled with Japanese messages; the volume indicated that a large-scale thrust was planned. But where? Studying the intercepts, Rochefort noted the repeated use of the letters AF. Whatever AF stood for, he guessed, was the Japanese objective.

Early in the war, Rochefort recalled, the Japanese code had used groups of two or three letters, each starting with A, to denote various Pacific locations. AH had turned out to be for Pearl Harbor; AG for French Frigate Shoals, where Japanese seaplanes had refueled from submarines. Rochefort remembered an intercepted message to those planes warning them to avoid a nearby place the sender called AF.

AF, Rochefort concluded, had to be Midway Island. Since the loss of Wake, the tiny atoll was the westernmost point in the Pacific where the United States flag still flew.

Some of Rochefort's superiors were skeptical. Prior to the Pearl Harbor attack, the Japanese had maintained a strict radio silence; why would they now send out signals concerning another major move? And suppose it were in the offing. Its objective might be the Aleutian Islands; many of the latest intercepts included letter groups known to represent locations there. The Japanese could be after bigger game than Midway: the Aleutians would give them a springboard for attacking Alaska, even California.

Rochefort proposed to test his thesis. With the approval of the Pacific Fleet's new Commander-in-Chief, Admiral Chester Nimitz, Midway was secretly ordered to send out a bogus message—in the clear—reporting the breakdown of

MIDWAY: THE TURNING POINT

its distillation plant. Two days later a new Japanese intercept reported that AF was short of fresh water.

Japan's primary target was indeed Midway, but Midway was only a means to an end. An attack on Midway, Tokyo reasoned, would be sure bait with which the U.S. Pacific Fleet could be lured into battle and annihilated.

However weakened by the strike at Pearl Harbor, the Pacific Fleet was still a menace to Japan's southern operations and, as Doolittle's carrier-based raid had demonstrated, could someday pose a massive threat to the Japanese homeland. The Pacific Fleet had to be destroyed now.

The battle plan conceived by Admiral Yamamoto, the formidable Commander-in-Chief of the Imperial Combined Fleet, called for an even greater armada than the one used in the Pearl Harbor attack: eight carriers, 11 battleships, 20 cruisers, 60 destroyers, 15 submarines, some 30 auxiliary vessels and 16 transports. Air power was to be supplied by more than 700 planes, both carrier- and island-based.

To deploy this mighty assemblage required the intricate sort of scheme of which Yamamoto was particularly fond. Submarines would move out first to form a picket line between Hawaii and Midway, scouting all ship movements westward from Pearl Harbor. Next, a diversionary Northern Force would launch an air raid on the American base at Dutch Harbor in the Aleutians, then seize and occupy Kiska and Attu, the westernmost islands of the chain. While the Americans focused on the Aleutians, planes of the First Carrier Striking Force would smash Midway's defenses, so that transports could land their 5,000 troops. Finally, when the Pacific Fleet steamed out of Pearl Harbor to the rescue, Yamamoto's Main Force, lurking several hundred miles away, would join the warships already at Midway and together they would blow the Americans out of the water. Yamamoto's flagship alone, the *Yamato*—at 69,100 tons the world's biggest battleship—could hurl 13 tons of steel more than 25 miles in one broadside from its 18.1-inch guns.

Yamamoto had the cream of the Japanese Navy and Naval Air Force at his disposal. Vice Admiral Chuichi Nagumo, who had commanded the Pearl Harbor attack, led the First Carrier Striking Force. Aboard his flagship, the 34,000-ton carrier *Akagi*, was Commander Minoru Genda, the operations specialist Yamamoto had recalled from attaché duty in London to oversee the Pearl Harbor plan.

As May waned, Yamamoto confidently sent his armada to sea. The odds seemed overwhelming. The Americans had only three carriers to oppose his eight, eight cruisers to his 20, 14 destroyers to his 60. They did have a slight edge in submarines—19 to his 15. But against his 11 battleships they had none: six U.S. battleships had survived Pearl Harbor but all were too damaged to use. On Midway the Americans had only about 100 planes to meet Yamamoto's 650 or so, and their pilots were mostly untested in combat.

But there was much that Yamamoto did not know. The Japanese strike at Pearl Harbor had not been the unmitigated disaster Americans back home believed it to be. The attackers had completely ignored the repair facilities of the naval base and the vital tank farm, where 4.5 million barrels of fuel oil were stored. Had these installations and supplies been destroyed, the Pacific Fleet would have been forced to withdraw to the West Coast. Moreover, not a single carrier had been struck; by chance they were all away at the time.

In one other important respect, Yamamoto's confidence was misplaced. His latest information about the enemy's carriers was wrong. Faulty intelligence reports had declared both the *Yorktown* and the *Lexington* sunk in the recent Coral Sea battle; the *Yorktown*, though badly damaged, had survived. Two other American carriers, the *Hornet* and the *Enterprise*, were said by Japanese intelligence to be operating near the Solomon Islands, far from Midway.

So far as Yamamoto knew, no enemy carriers would show up to challenge his own. Therefore, he felt safe in dispersing his ships. His force was divided into 10 groups, separated from one another by hundreds of miles. They were vulnerable even to a numerically inferior foe—and especially one forewarned of their movements.

On May 26 the *Hornet* and the *Enterprise*, believed by Yamamoto to be in the South Pacific, loomed over the horizon at Pearl Harbor with the rest of the ships of Task Force 16; Nimitz had ordered them back on the double. On the 27th, the battered *Yorktown* limped in at the head of Task Force 17, trailing a 10-mile oil slick. The *Yorktown*'s skipper had estimated she would need about 90 days to be put back into shape. Nimitz gave him 72 hours.

On Midway, 1,150 miles to the west, preparations had also been stepped up. Bunkers arose in the atoll's sands, tunnels were dug, miles of concertina wire were strung, tons of antipersonnel mines were buried in the beaches, antiaircraft batteries rushed from Hawaii were emplaced.

Midway's 37 obsolete aircraft were reinforced by the best the Navy could spare: 30 Catalina patrol bombers and 32 carrier castoffs, among them Wildcat fighters, Avenger torpedo planes and Dauntless dive bombers. The Army sent in four B-26 Marauders, which were rigged for torpedoes, and 15 high-level B-17s.

Soon planes packed the runways, and the Catalinas were extending their reconnaissance range to 700 miles. Though the patrols would be of crucial aid to the American carriers in finding the enemy armada, Nimitz warned Midway's defenders that they could expect no help from the carriers in return. Midway was on its own. Come what may, the carriers would have to stay in hiding until Nagumo's First Carrier Striking Force steamed into the trap.

As conceived by its planners, the trap was simple: while planes of Nagumo's four carriers were off attacking Midway, planes of the three United States carriers would swoop in to wreak havoc on the enemy carriers themselves.

On May 28, two days after Nagumo's force left Tokyo Bay and moved eastward, the *Hornet*, the *Enterprise* and the six cruisers and nine destroyers of Task Force 16 left Pearl Harbor and moved westward. During its two days in port, Task Force 16 had changed leaders. Vice Admiral William ("Bull") Halsey lay in the base hospital, at doctor's orders; during six hazardous months at sea, the boldest of Nimitz's commanders had lost 20 pounds and acquired an agonizing case of dermatitis. Temporarily replacing Halsey was Rear Admiral Raymond Spruance, who had directed his cruisers. Spruance had no carrier experience, but he was a meticulous technician with a swift, slide-rule intellect and, as events would prove, a capacity for command decision.

Task Force 17—the *Yorktown*, two cruisers and five destroyers—filed out of harbor on May 30. On the *Yorktown*'s bridge stood Rear Admiral Frank Jack Fletcher, in tactical charge of both task forces.

On June 2, the forces rendezvoused at a position hopefully dubbed "Point Luck," 325 miles northeast of Midway. En route, selected officers had been shown a remarkably precise document, prepared by Nimitz's chief intelligence aide, Lieut. Commander Edward Layton, forecasting the enemy's plans for Midway, including the direction from which Nagu-

mo's carriers would come ("from the northwest on bearing 325°") and the point where they would be sighted ("about 175 miles from Midway"). One astonished officer could not believe the material had been prepared at a desk in Pearl Harbor. "That man of ours in Tokyo," he said, "is worth every cent we pay him."

While Task Forces 16 and 17 lay waiting for Nagumo's carriers to come within range of aerial ambush, a third United States force, under Rear Admiral Robert Theobald, rode the waters of the Gulf of Alaska. Theobald thought a Japanese thrust at the Aleutians unlikely. As he saw it, those perpetually fog-bound islets were hardly worth the enemy's effort. Theobald scented a ruse. The actual target in the area, he suspected, would be Alaska itself. And so he positioned his cruisers and destroyers where he thought they would do the most good: off the Alaskan mainland.

As an American naval historian later put it, Theobald's force "proved about as useful as if it had been in the South Atlantic." It was more than 500 miles away when, at dawn on June 3, the United States base at Dutch Harbor in the eastern Aleutians took a hail of Japanese bombs from 12 planes off the *Ryujo,* one of the two carriers of Yamamoto's diversionary Northern Force. The attackers leveled the base barracks, killing 25 of the occupants.

Word of the enemy operations in the Aleutians, sent out by the base radio and picked up by American monitors, gave Nimitz his first alert. The second came just a few hours

Lieut. Commander Joseph J. Rochefort, whose brilliant decoding of Japanese messages helped the United States win the Battle of Midway, enlisted in the Navy during World War I, became a machinist in 1919 and was commissioned as an ensign that same year.

later. At 9 a.m. a young ensign named Jewell Reid, piloting a Catalina at the outer limits of its patrol 700 miles southwest of Midway, sighted a large number of ships heading his way. Reid flashed a terse message by radio to Midway—"Main body"—then spent two hours diving in and out of clouds, observing as much as he could. After he had counted 11 enemy ships, Midway ordered him back to base.

Meanwhile other Catalinas had sighted ships in the same general area, and nine Flying Fortresses roared out of Midway to the attack. It was late afternoon before the high-altitude B-17s reached the enemy ships and dropped their bombs. Back at base, they reported hitting two battleships or heavy cruisers and two transports; in fact, they hit nothing. After nightfall four Catalinas, carrying torpedoes, returned to the assault; they damaged one tanker.

As the cables from Midway streamed into Pearl Harbor, Nimitz realized what Midway's defenders did not: that the ships their planes had attacked were part of the Japanese invasion force out of Saipan, southwest of Midway. It was not the "main body"; apparently it did not even include carriers. The real prize, Admiral Nagumo's First Carrier Striking Force, was yet to appear, and when it did it would come from the northwest.

Fearing that Fletcher and Spruance might have picked up Reid's radio flash to Midway, Nimitz relayed it to them, with the warning: "That is not, repeat not, the enemy's strike force." That night, Task Forces 16 and 17 moved from Point Luck to a point some 200 miles north of Midway.

Admiral Nagumo, meanwhile, was speeding toward Midway from the northwest, with no information except what his search planes could provide. Though word of the spotting of the transports from Saipan had reached Yamamoto, he could not inform Nagumo without risk of revealing his own position to American radio monitors.

Nor was Nagumo aware that the submarines assigned to reconnaissance between Hawaii and Midway had arrived too late; thanks to advance knowledge of the Japanese plans, Task Forces 16 and 17 had already slipped past.

At dawn on June 4, in the ready rooms of the First Carrier Striking Force, Nagumo's pilots partook of dry chestnuts and cold *sake*, traditional fare for warriors about to go into battle. Topside, half of Nagumo's planes sat on the bright-yellow flight deck, ready to start up. Below, the other half were being armed with torpedoes for the American ships expected to react to the assault.

The first faint streaks of light lay on the horizon as the carrier ritual began. Alarms clanged. The *Akagi* turned into the wind. Bull horns blared, "Pilots, man your planes." The thunder of 108 engines roared out over the ocean. One by one, the planes lurched forward, rumbled into the brightening air, and sped away.

At 5:34 a.m. Lieutenant Howard Ady, piloting a Catalina about an hour out of Midway, spotted the Japanese carriers and reported planes heading for Midway. At 5:53, the island's radar spotted the planes 93 miles away. In 20 minutes, every Midway plane was in the air. The bombers headed toward the Japanese carriers. There were no fewer than four: the *Akagi,* the *Kaga,* the *Soryu* and the *Hiryu.*

Meanwhile, orbiting high above Midway, its six Wildcat and 20 Buffalo fighters pounced on the incoming Japanese bombers from above and shot down three of them. But as the fighters clawed for altitude, the swifter Zero escort swooped in. In 25 minutes, 17 of Midway's fighters were shot down and seven others were forced out of action.

Nagumo's planes—108 dive bombers, torpedo bombers and Zeroes—roared over the island like a typhoon. Midway's antiaircraft opened up, and some Japanese planes burst into flames. But the bombs rained down. Of the island's 3,000 defenders, 24 were killed and 18 wounded; the seaplane hangar and a fuel dump exploded; the powerhouse, dispensary and water-processing plant were demolished. But when the last Zero completed its strafing run and disappeared out to sea, Midway's runways and antiaircraft batteries were still in action. Flight leader Joichi Tomonaga radioed Nagumo: "Second strike needed."

Nagumo had arrived at that conclusion on his own. In about two hours, his fleet had withstood five separate onslaughts by Midway's bombers. Antiaircraft fire hurled up by the screening ships, combined with the Zeroes' deadly gunfire, had taken a gratifying toll. Seven of 10 American torpedo planes and eight dive bombers had gone down; not one scored a hit on a ship.

But Nagumo could not rest easy. Most of the enemy's bombers had escaped unharmed. They had to be destroyed if Midway was to be taken. He ordered that the torpedo planes he had reserved to deal with any nearby enemy ships be rearmed with bombs. It would take about an hour.

At 7:28 a.m., half of Nagumo's bombers were ready for takeoff to Midway when a Japanese search plane completing the last leg of its patrol reported a sighting: "Ten enemy surface ships."

At first Nagumo felt a flicker of satisfaction; the Pacific Fleet had finally risen to the Japanese Navy's bait! Then a chilling thought occurred to the admiral: if, contrary to earlier reports, the American ships included a carrier, his own fleet was now within range of its planes. Nagumo frantically tried to find out—and got silence from his search plane. Then, at 8:09, the pilot reported again: "Five cruisers, five destroyers." Nagumo sighed in relief. But at 8:20 the search plane reported a third time: "Enemy carrier appears to be bringing up the rear."

The news struck Nagumo like a sledge. He had thrown every one of his Zeroes into the air to fight off the planes attacking from Midway. Almost all his torpedo planes had been rearmed with bombs. Nagumo now ordered them changed back to torpedoes—thus losing another precious hour. In their haste, the crews made a fateful mistake: they left the unshackled bombs on deck.

At this point a new complication arose. Flight leader Tomonaga and his first wave of Midway raiders, shot up and low on fuel, appeared overhead urgently requesting permission to land on the carrier decks.

Every minute that Nagumo lost in launching his attack on the United States carrier brought its planes closer to him. Yet he vacillated. Pacing the Akagi's bridge, he turned to the operations specialist, Commander Genda, whose judgment was tantamount to Yamamoto's, and Genda quietly made the decision for him: first recover the Midway raiders and their Zero escort before they were forced down at sea. Next re-form the scattered ships and close with the enemy fleet. Then, as originally planned, mount an all-out air attack that would devastate the Pacific Fleet.

On the Enterprise, Spruance made some quick calculations. His radio had picked up Catalina pilot Ady's message to Midway at 5:34 a.m., the first report of the sighting of Nagumo's carriers. On orders from Fletcher, Spruance had rushed Task Force 16 on ahead while Fletcher waited for the return of Task Force 17's dawn patrol. Spruance now reckoned that within three hours he would be within 100 miles of Nagumo's fleet, a striking distance from which his fighters could operate comfortably. But in three hours, Spruance knew, he might lose the only real advantage he had: surprise. He would have to risk his planes.

Spruance risked every one of them. At 7:02 a.m., with the Japanese still at a distance of some 170 miles—the American fighters' maximum range—the man who had never before commanded a carrier launched all 67 dive bombers, all 29 torpedo planes and all 20 fighters off the Enterprise and the Hornet. About two hours later, aboard the Yorktown, Fletcher sent out a squadron of 12 torpedo bombers and a strike group of 17 dive bombers and six fighters.

From the Hornet, 35 dive bombers and 10 fighters raced to the projected intercept point, only to find nothing, for Nagumo had headed northeast to hunt the Pacific Fleet. The Hornet's planes turned south toward Midway and never found Nagumo's ships. Two squadrons off the Enterprise, Bombing 6 and Scouting 6, under Lieut. Commander Wade McClusky, did not find them at the intercept point either. But McClusky turned his planes toward open sea instead of toward Midway and went looking for the enemy.

Meanwhile Torpedo 8, off the Hornet, found Nagumo's carriers. But the squadron's fighter cover had set off toward Midway with the Hornet's first 35 bombers. A swarm of Zeroes dived on the unescorted torpedo planes and shot them down. A few of the American planes were able to fire their torpedoes; they missed.

Torpedo 6, off the Enterprise, followed the Hornet group in. The squadron's leader, Lieut. Commander Gene Lindsey, had fighters, but they were stacked up above a cloud cover at 14,000 feet awaiting his call to action. The call never came. Zeroes gunned down 10 of the bombers, including Lindsey's. The other four dropped their torpedoes and got away, but these missiles, too, missed.

Torpedo 3, off the Yorktown, found Nagumo's fleet next. An escort of six Wildcat fighters, under Lieut. Commander Jimmy Thach, fought furiously and shot down a number of Zeroes, but more kept coming. As Thach said later: "It was like the inside of a beehive." Down below, still more Zeroes pounced on Torpedo 3's incoming planes. One by one, seven were blown up. Five others managed to release their

Pilots of the U.S. aircraft carrier Hornet's new and untried Torpedo Squadron 8 gather for a picture on the flight deck before taking off to attack Japanese carriers in the Battle of Midway. Only one squadron member—Ensign George Gay (front row, fourth from left)—survived the action that followed. Shot down as he attacked the carrier Akagi, he clung to a raft and watched the rest of the battle from the water.

torpedoes; all missed. Then three of these five planes were knocked down trying to break clear.

All that remained of the 200 or so planes from the American carrier force were 54 planes.

Nagumo's spirits were improving. In three hours, his ships had faced no fewer than eight American air attacks. Yet except for minor strafing damage, not one of his ships had been hit. Meanwhile, he had recovered and refueled 93 of his own planes and readied them for takeoff. Now, Nagumo reflected with satisfaction, it was his turn to attack. At 10:24 a.m. the first Zero zoomed off the *Akagi's* deck.

Just then, lookouts on the *Akagi* and the *Kaga* yelled in unison: "Enemy dive bombers!" Crewmen stared in disbelief. High above, little gray planes with white stars on their wings were peeling off, one by one, and hurtling down toward them. Not one of Nagumo's covering Zeroes was high enough to deter the newcomers; they had been maneuvering at low altitude to stop the American torpedo bombers.

On the *Akagi's* flight deck was standing Commander Mitsuo Fuchida, the leader of Japan's strike at Pearl Harbor. Now he learned what it was like to be on the wrong end. "Black objects suddenly floated eerily from their wings," he recalled. "Bombs! Down they came, straight toward me!" Fuchida scrambled for safety, broke both ankles while leaping from one deck to another.

As quickly as the strike had come, it was over. A huge crater gaped amidships on the flight deck. The plane elevator was exposed, drooping and twisting, Fuchida said, "like molten glass." But the bombs had only started the havoc. With the *Akagi* turned into the wind for takeoffs, flames swirled aft, ignited the wooden flight deck and engulfed the bunched-up planes, setting off their fuel tanks and the torpedoes slung beneath them.

Then the bombs that had been carelessly left stacked on deck began exploding. Fire fighters were blown to pieces. On the bridge, an officer burst in, choking with smoke, to report: "All passageways below are afire. The only way out is by rope, from the window of the bridge."

Nagumo stood transfixed, staring at the fires. In his long career, he had never lost a ship. Finally an aide took his hand, and Nagumo nodded assent. A rope was flung from the leeward screen. Nagumo, with Fuchida close behind, lowered himself to the burning flight deck, scrambled to the anchor deck and stepped aboard the launch waiting to transfer him to the cruiser *Nagara,* away from the hulk that had been his flagship.

The devastation was much the same aboard the carriers *Soryu* and *Kaga.* Fully 34 of Wade McClusky's 37 planes had plastered the *Kaga.* Four direct hits sent flames raging through the torpedo magazines. The resulting explosions

blew away a sizable portion of the ship and its crew and left it, as one sailor recalled, "like a skull smashed open."

The *Soryu* was the victim of Bombing Squadron 3, off the *Yorktown*. Lieut. Commander Max Leslie aimed at the Rising Sun emblem on the foredeck, and let his bomb fly. Two other bombs hit, and the entire ship burst into flames. The third of Nagumo's four great carriers was done for.

But the last carrier, the *Hiryu*, was very much alive. At 10:40 a.m. 18 dive bombers and six Zeroes rumbled off its deck to seek revenge. Flight leader Lieutenant Michio Kobayashi, another Pearl Harbor veteran, cannily tailed some returning American planes straight to the *Yorktown*.

At 30 miles out, 12 Wildcats of the *Yorktown*'s Combat Air Patrol fell on the Japanese bombers from above and dropped 10 of them into the sea. Kobayashi and his seven remaining bomber pilots broke free, bored through the wall of antiaircraft fire sent up by the *Yorktown*'s screening ships and dived on the carrier. Her guns roared and Kobayashi's plane blew up. But its bomb dropped and exploded on the carrier's flight deck in a hail of deadly fragments.

A number of planes on the hangar deck caught fire; quick use of the sprinkler system beat back that danger. A second bomb slammed through the forward elevator and exploded deep below, threatening the ammunition magazines and a high-octane fuel compartment. That menace was averted when the magazines were flooded with sea water and the gasoline locker was swathed in carbon dioxide.

Then a third bomb exploded inside of the *Yorktown*'s smokestacks. It tore up the exhausts, knocked out five of the ship's six boilers and left her dead in the water.

Only six Japanese planes survived the attack. But one of them got off the message to Nagumo that helped assuage his losses: "Enemy carrier burning!"

At 1 p.m. Fletcher transferred his flag to the cruiser *Astoria* and radioed Nimitz that Task Force 17 would stand by to protect the *Yorktown*, thus relinquishing tactical command of the battle to Spruance. Fletcher had just left the *Yorktown* when engine-room repair crews got her boilers working again. She inched forward and by 2 p.m., to the cheers of her crew, the battered carrier was up to 20 knots.

But a second Japanese attack was coming. Ten torpedo bombers and six Zeroes—all the *Hiryu*'s remaining planes—streaked in. For their leader, Joichi Tomonaga, it was the

second mission of the day. He knew it would be his last. That morning, over Midway, his wing tank had been hit; now he had only enough fuel for a one-way trip.

Tomonaga made the most of it. While his Zeroes tangled with the *Yorktown*'s fighters, he split his bombers to come in on both sides of the ship, bringing them in only yards off the water. He got his own torpedo away, but in the next instant his plane took a hit and exploded. The *Yorktown* swerved hard to port; Tomonaga's torpedo missed. But he had set up the kill. Moments later, two torpedoes punched into the *Yorktown*'s port side. Oil gushed from ruptured fuel tanks. Sea water flooded in. The carrier's power went out again and she listed 17°.

At 3 p.m. Captain Elliott Buckmaster gave the order to abandon ship. Then he toured the darkened interior, satisfied himself that no one was left down there alive, stepped off into the sea and swam to an approaching launch.

For three hours, United States planes had been hunting for Nagumo's last remaining carrier. Minutes before the *Yorktown* received her deathblow, word came from one of her search planes off to the west: 10 enemy ships steaming north, with a carrier right in the middle of them.

Around 3:30 p.m., 24 planes—everything Spruance could sweep up, including 10 refugee dive bombers from the *Yorktown*—sped away from the *Enterprise*. An hour and a half later the flight leader, Lieutenant Earl Gallaher, spotted the telltale wakes and circled around to the west to attack out of the lowering sun.

As Gallaher's planes winged over into their dives on the *Hiryu*, the last few Zeroes of Nagumo's fleet, fighting now to save their last flight deck, followed them down. They blasted three of the American bombers to pieces, tore holes in several others and threw the attackers into such confusion that no one could say whose planes scored the hits.

Four big bombs slammed home. The *Hiryu*'s planes blew up. The forward third of the flight deck became a mass of flames. For more than seven hours, the carrier's crew struggled to save her. But just before midnight, the heat of the fires touched off an explosion that blew out the ship's insides. The *Hiryu* lurched over 15° and Captain Tomeo Kaku ordered the ship abandoned.

In the light of the burning flight deck, Admiral Tamon Yamaguchi, the brilliant officer who had been deemed most likely to succeed Yamamoto himself and who was in command of two of the Japanese carriers at Midway, addressed the 800 or so men who were about to leave the stricken *Hiryu*. "I am fully and solely responsible for the loss of the *Hiryu* and *Soryu*," he told them. "I shall remain on board until the end." He handed his black cap to an aide as a memento, radioed an apology to Nagumo and poured a farewell toast from a beaker of water. The flag of the Rising Sun fluttered down. Bugles sounded the Japanese national anthem. A portrait of the Emperor was reverently passed to a destroyer standing by. As the crewmen left the ship, Yamaguchi issued his last order to the screening destroyers: "Torpedo and sink the *Hiryu*." With flames licking at the bridge, the admiral turned to Captain Kaku and said calmly, "Let us enjoy the beauty of the moon."

Yamamoto, still hundreds of miles to the west on the superbattleship *Yamato*, saw that his grand design had gone awry. Just after noon, upon learning that three of Nagumo's four carriers were burning, Yamamoto began reshuffling his fleet in a final effort to reverse its fortunes.

A flurry of orders went forth. The Midway invasion force was to get out of the way. Half a dozen battleships, four heavy cruisers and a submarine were to shell Midway's runways. All other fighting ships—including the Aleutian force—were to go after the U.S. Fleet.

It was too late. The Aleutian force would take at least a day to arrive. The warships of the invasion covering force could not possibly get within bombardment range of Midway before 3 a.m. on June 5. And once the sun came up, American aircraft would be upon Yamamoto's ships again.

At last Yamamoto had to face the reality of his defeat. At 2:55 a.m. on June 5 he ordered all commands to join him several hundred miles to the west. "The price," he was heard to whisper, "is too high." The first line of his message to his fleet read, "The Midway occupation is canceled."

Contact between the foes was not yet ended. Early in the morning of June 5, the American submarine *Tambor* sighted a column of retiring Japanese warships and was sighted by them. As they took evasive action, the cruisers *Mogami* and *Mikuma* collided. Next day Spruance's planes found the crippled ships, sank the *Mikuma* and so damaged the *Mogami* that she was put out of action for a year.

The same day, the Japanese caught up with the *Yorktown* while she was under tow alongside the destroyer *Hammann*. Torpedoes from a Japanese sub sank the *Hammann* and hit the *Yorktown*. She sank the next morning, as one account put it, "like a tired colossus, hurt beyond pain."

In the Aleutians on June 6, Japanese naval units occupied Kiska. Next day a Japanese Army battalion landed on Attu. Both landings were unopposed. The invaders were to cling to their isolated and useless outposts until the Americans finally got around to ousting them in mid-1943.

The sweeping extent of the American victory at Midway could be known only in later years. The Japanese Navy was never to recover from the battle. Yamamoto would never again return to the offensive. For his country, there would be no new conquests except in China; instead, there would be an increasingly desperate defense of spoils already won.

As a deeply dejected and humiliated Yamamoto turned his ships homeward on June 7, he could only guess at the future; but the present was grim enough. His ill-fated venture had cost four carriers, one cruiser, 322 planes, and the lives of 3,500 Japanese fighting men, including 100 irreplaceable first-line pilots. The Americans had lost a carrier, a destroyer, 150 planes and 307 lives.

The Japanese people were not told of the crushing defeat they had suffered; only the Aleutian landings were trumpeted. The return of the men wounded in the Midway operation was shrouded in secrecy. Among them was Commander Fuchida, who had been hailed six months earlier by his countrymen as the hero of the Pearl Harbor strike.

As a result of the broken ankles he had sustained on the *Akagi*, Fuchida had been transferred to a hospital ship. When it put in at the Yokosuka naval base, he later wrote, "I was not moved ashore until after dark when the streets were deserted. I was taken to the hospital on a covered stretcher and carried through the rear entrance. My room was in complete isolation. No nurses or corpsmen were allowed in and I could not communicate with the outside. It was like being a prisoner of war among your own people."

Some highly placed Japanese were privy to the facts about Midway. One was Mamoru Shigemitsu, soon to become Japan's Foreign Minister. Shigemitsu put the truth about the battle succinctly. At Midway, he said later, "the Americans had avenged Pearl Harbor."

JAPAN'S AUDACIOUS GAMBLER

Fellow officers fete Admiral Isoroku Yamamoto (standing) in 1934 on his departure for London, where he renounced a treaty limiting the size of Japan's navy.

FAMILY ALBUM OF A FLAMBOYANT ADMIRAL

The naval genius entrusted by Japan with the vital task of smashing the U.S. Pacific Fleet was a many-sided man. In sharp contrast to most Japanese military leaders, Admiral Isoroku Yamamoto was an urbane world traveler who spoke fluent English, admired the United States and claimed many American friends. A patriot to the bone, he argued passionately for peace, but when ordered to fight he waged war with aggressive brilliance.

This son of a schoolmaster, born in 1884, got his first taste of combat in 1904, when he participated as an ensign in Admiral Heihachiro Togo's defeat of the Russian Fleet in the strait of Tsushima between Korea and Japan. In 1919 Commander Yamamoto, who was then 35 years old, was sent to Harvard University, where he studied English, mastered bridge and poker, and amused friends with his impromptu acrobatics (left).

In 1934 Yamamoto, by this time a vice admiral, served as Japan's chief delegate to the London Naval Conference, where he forced the termination by the end of 1936 of a treaty that had kept Japan's capital ship fleet inferior to those of Great Britain and America by a ratio of 5 to 3. Then, over the opposition of Japan's old-line battleship admirals, he successfully lobbied for the construction of aircraft carriers, whose key role he had foreseen as early as 1915. The officers under his command received vigorous, often unorthodox training; Yamamoto sometimes put tacks on the seats of their chairs as a reminder of the need for constant vigilance. An inveterate gambler, he made his aides learn poker as training in the arts of bluff and surprise.

On September 13, 1941, Yamamoto committed himself—and his country—to the greatest gamble of his career. The success of his long-shot carrier attack against the American base at Pearl Harbor made him an overnight hero, even to those Japanese who had earlier assailed his pleas for peace. But Yamamoto knew that even the luckiest streak runs out. "The sinking of four or five battleships," he wrote to a sister, "is no cause for celebration. There will be times of defeat as well as victory."

A headstand, like this one at the home of an American friend in 1920, was one of Yamamoto's favorite devices for breaking the ice at social affairs.

大正七年八月卅日

五十六

禮子

On a 1918 photograph of Lieutenant Yamamoto and his bride, Hiroko, a dairyman's daughter, the groom inscribed their names and the wedding date.

Most Americans Yamamoto met in the United States took to him as readily as did these smiling children of Waltham, Massachusetts, who were photographed

with him while he was a student at Harvard.

Returning home via Berlin from London in 1934, Yamamoto (front row, third from left) is greeted by Japanese diplomats and German officials. Unlike many other high-ranking Japanese, he distrusted the Nazis.

Yamamoto pauses in 1926 in front of the Capitol in snowbound Washington, D.C., where he served as naval attaché and studied U.S. defense and shipbuilding programs.

A few days after the attack on Pearl Harbor, Admiral Yamamoto (above dot, front row) and his staff sit for a full-dress portrait on the flight deck of the carrier Akagi, whose torpedo planes helped cripple the U.S. Pacific Fleet. While still at sea, Yamamoto inscribed a letter to his wife and sons: "Glad to know you are all well. But take care, it's getting increasingly cold. I'm doing my best. It's war, and I wouldn't know what might happen to me. But I have no time to think about such things. Indeed, this is the crucial period that might decide victory or defeat for Japan."

AN ALL-OUT THRUST AT HOME

A retired general shows uniformed instructors and members of the Patriotic Women's Association in Mito how to wield a bamboo spear to repel invaders.

DEDICATION TO NIPPON'S DESTINY

On the clear, bitingly cold morning of Monday, December 8, 1941, Japanese civilians returned to their jobs with a sense of dedication and destiny. By a brilliant tactical surprise, their Navy's airmen had just smashed the United States Pacific Fleet, and Japan was committed to a global war. It was true that the Japanese had been on a war footing since their invasion of China in 1937. But now every citizen was being called upon to devote himself to the war effort for the glory of the Emperor.

With virtually all able-bodied young men in the armed services, women laid aside their traditional kimonos in the months that followed, donned drab blouses and baggy pants called *monpe,* and took over the men's jobs in steel mills, coal mines and munitions factories. Children unloaded freight cars and worked as riveters in aircraft factories. Retired Army officers were mobilized to show civilians how to combat potential invaders. Even monk power was utilized: several thousand Buddhist monks were conscripted, divested of their robes and sent to work in munitions plants. Other monks aided a national scrap-metal drive that collected everything from radiators to park benches.

In the cities, neighborhoods erupted with realistic air raid drills, as fire wardens started blazes to train the populace in putting out fires. Every inch of arable land, including public parks and even Tokyo's Olympic Stadium, was used to grow food. Bustling and gaudy city thoroughfares gradually fell silent; since most gasoline was earmarked for the military, only bicycles and a few smoky, charcoal-burning cars traversed the streets.

For the most part, Japanese civilians bore their sacrifices cheerfully, imbued as they were with the martial spirit of *banzai*—victory. Moreover, they knew that Japan had powerful allies—Germany and Italy—and their own government had assured them that the only real shortages were in America. Buoyed by unlimited faith in their national destiny, a crowd of Japanese rousingly cheered a visiting Italian official who said: "For Americans, it is the dollar that is the moving spirit. They cannot win."

Students in Tokyo show off a class project: a paper Nazi fish devouring General Maurice Gamelin, the commander of France's defeated Army.

German, Italian and Japanese flags deck the Ginza, Tokyo's main shopping street, to celebrate the 1936 signing of a tripartite anti-Communist pact.

By the light of a single electric bulb, bare-breasted women join men in the grimy chore of mining the coal that fueled Japan's wartime industry.

Women and children load baskets with charcoal, which was to be sold for cooking, heating and powering civilian vehicles.

A squad of women in baggy work trousers pulls a load of earth from a bomb shelter being built under a Tokyo residential area.

Using every piece of arable land, farm hands tend cattle and crops in a Tokyo stadium built for the aborted 1940 Olympic Games.

Pumpkin vines ramble over shacks in a Tokyo slum. Food shortages made easily-grown pumpkins so ubiquitous that the Japanese grew heartily sick of them.

"I too will help destroy the Americans and the English," says a banner on a Tokyo lamppost slated to be melted down for weapons. Scrap-metal drives, launched well before Pearl Harbor, denuded cities of lampposts, statues, bridge railings and park benches.

Buddhist monks strain to move a heavy temple bell into place at a scrap-metal collection depot. The bells, many of them centuries-old masterpieces, were rounded up from temples all over Japan.

Workers prepare to carry away a radiator after using the hammers in the foreground to break it away from its steampipe.

Students waving Japanese flags trek through snow to Tokyo's
Imperial Palace to celebrate the defeat of the British at Singapore.

One-legged war veterans hobble up the lower slopes of Mount Fuji, the
snow-capped sacred volcano near Tokyo. The Japanese believed that
the mountain climb purified the body. For these victims of the war, it was
also a gesture for the Emperor and the greater glory of Japan.

BIBLIOGRAPHY

Attiwill, Kenneth, *Fortress*. Doubleday & Co., Inc., 1960.

Barker, A. J., *Yamashita*. Ballantine Books Inc., 1973.

Beck, John Jacob, *MacArthur and Wainwright: Sacrifice of the Philippines*. University of New Mexico Press, 1974.

Belote, James H. and William M. Belote, *Corregidor: The Saga of a Fortress*. Harper & Row, 1967.

Benda, Harry J., *The Crescent and the Rising Sun*. W. van Hoeve Ltd., 1958.

Benedict, Ruth, *The Chrysanthemum and the Sword*. Houghton Mifflin Company, 1946.

Bergamini, David, *Japan's Imperial Conspiracy*. William Morrow and Company, Inc., 1971.

Borton, Hugh, *Japan's Modern Century*. The Ronald Press Company, 1970.

Brereton, Lewis H., *The Brereton Diaries*. William Morrow and Company, 1946.

Butow, Robert J. C., *Tojo and the Coming of the War*. Princeton University Press, 1961.

Churchill, Winston S., *The Second World War*, Vol. 3: *The Grand Alliance*. Cassell & Co., Ltd., 1950.

Collier, Basil, *The War in the Far East, 1941-1945*. William Morrow and Company, Inc., 1969.

Congdon, Don, ed., *Combat: The War with Japan*. Dell Publishing Co., Inc., 1962.

Craven, Wesley Frank and James Lea Cate, eds., *The Army Air Forces in World War II*, Vol. 1: *Plans and Early Operations*. The University of Chicago Press, 1948.

Cunningham, W. Scott, *Wake Island Command*. Little, Brown and Company, 1961.

Devereux, James P. S., *The Story of Wake Island*. J. P. Lippincott Co., 1947.

Dupuy, R. Ernest, *The Compact History of the United States Army*. Hawthorn Books, Inc., 1961.

Esposito, Vincent J., ed., *The West Point Atlas of American Wars*, Vol. 2: *1900-1953*. Frederick A. Praeger, 1960.

Feis, Herbert, *The Road to Pearl Harbor*. Atheneum, 1965.

Fuchida, Mitsuo and Masatake Okumiya, *Midway, The Battle that Doomed Japan*. Ballantine Books, 1968.

Gordon, Ernest, *Through the Valley of the Kwai*. Harper & Brothers, 1962.

Grew, Joseph C., *Ten Years in Japan*. Simon and Schuster, 1944.

Gunnison, Royal Arch, *So Sorry, No Peace*. The Viking Press, 1944.

Hough, Lieut. Colonel Frank O., Major Verle E. Ludwig and Henry I. Shaw Jr., *Pearl Harbor to Guadalcanal*. U.S. Marine Corps (no date).

Hull, Cordell, *Memoirs*. The Macmillan Company, 1948.

Ike, Nobutaka, ed., *Japan's Decision for War*. Stanford University Press, 1967.

Jablonski, Edward, *Flying Fortress*. Doubleday & Company, Inc., 1965.

Japan. Editors of FORTUNE Magazine, Time Inc., 1944.

The Japanese Navy in World War II. U.S. Naval Institute Proceedings, 1969.

Jones, F. C., *Japan's New Order in East Asia*. Oxford University Press, 1954.

Kabin, George McTurnan, *Nationalism and Revolution in Indonesia*. Cornell University Press, 1952.

Karig, Captain Walter and Commander Eric Purdon, *Battle Report, Pacific War: Middle Phase*. Rinehart and Company, Inc., 1947.

Kase, Toshikazu, *Journey to the "Missouri."* Yale University Press, 1950.

Keith, Agnes Newton, *Three Came Home*. Little, Brown and Company, 1947.

Kirby, Major-General S. Woodburn, *The War Against Japan*, Vols. 1 and 2. Her Majesty's Stationery Office, 1957.

Langer, William L. and S. Everett Gleason, *The Undeclared War, 1940-1941*. Peter Smith, 1968.

Latourette, Kenneth S., *A Short History of the Far East*. The Macmillan Company, 1964.

Leasor, James, *Singapore*. Doubleday & Company, Inc., 1968.

Lord, Walter:
  Day of Infamy. Holt, Rinehart and Winston, 1967.
  Incredible Victory. Harper & Row, Publishers, 1967.

MacArthur, Douglas, *Reminiscences*. McGraw-Hill Book Company, 1964.

Maw, Ba, *Breakthrough in Burma*. Yale University Press, 1968.

McDougall, William, Jr., *By Eastern Windows*. Charles Scribner's Sons, 1949.

Mellnik, Steve, *Philippine Diary, 1939-1945*. Van Nostrand Reinhold Company, 1969.

Millis, Walter, *This Is Pearl!* William Morrow and Company, 1947.

Mitchell, Donald W., *History of the Modern American Navy*. Alfred A. Knopf, 1946.

Morison, Samuel Eliot:
  History of United States Naval Operations in World War II, Vol. 3: *The Rising Sun in the Pacific*. Little, Brown and Company, 1975.
  History of United States Naval Operations in World War II, Vol. 4: *Coral Sea, Midway and Submarine Actions*. Little, Brown and Company, 1971.

Morton, Louis:
  The Fall of the Philippines. Department of the Army, 1973.
  United States Army in World War II, The War in the Pacific. Strategy and Command: The First Two Years. Department of the Army, 1962.

Mydans, Carl, *More than Meets the Eye*. Harper & Brothers, 1959.

Potter, E. B.:
  Nimitz. Naval Institute Press, 1976.
  United States Navy. Thomas Y. Crowell Company, 1971.

Potter, John Deane, *Yamamoto, The Man Who Menaced America*. The Viking Press, 1965.

Pouillard, Stanley S., *Bamboo Doctor*. St. Martin's Press, 1960.

Purcell, Victor, *South and East Asia Since 1800*. Cambridge University Press, 1965.

Reischauer, Edwin O., *Japan Past and Present*. Alfred A. Knopf, 1964.

Russell, Lord, of Liverpool, *The Knights of Bushido: The Shocking History of Japanese War Atrocities*. E. P. Dutton & Co., 1958.

Sakai, Saburo, Martin Caidin and Fred Saito, *Samurai!* E. P. Dutton & Co., 1957.

Shigemitsu, Mamoru, *Japan and Her Destiny*. E. P. Dutton & Co., 1958.

Smith, S. E., ed., *The United States Marine Corps in World War II*. Ace Books, 1973.

Stamps, T. Dodson and Vincent J. Esposito, eds., *A Military History of World War II*, Vol. 2: *Operations in the Mediterranean and Pacific Theaters*. United States Military Academy, 1956.

Steinberg, David Joel, *Philippine Collaboration in World War II*. The University of Michigan Press, 1967.

Stevens, Frederic H., *Santo Tomás* (no publisher, no date).

Storry, Richard, *A History of Modern Japan*. Penguin Books, 1960.

Taylor, George E., *The Philippines and the United States: Problems of Partnership*. Frederick A. Praeger, 1964.

Taylor, John W. R. and Kenneth Munson, *History of Aviation*. Crown Publishers, Inc., 1972.

Toland, John:
  But Not in Shame. Random House, 1961.
  The Rising Sun. Random House, 1970.

Tsuji, Masanobu, *Singapore, the Japanese Version*. St. Martin's Press, 1961.

Tuchman, Barbara, *Stilwell and the American Experience in China*. The Macmillan Company, 1971.

Tuleja, Commander Thaddeus, *Climax at Midway*. W. W. Norton & Company, Inc., 1960.

Wainwright, Jonathan M., *General Wainwright's Story*. Doubleday & Company, Inc., 1946.

Winslow, Walter, *Ghost of the Java Coast*. Coral Reef, 1974.

Wohlstetter, Roberta, *Pearl Harbor: Warning and Decision*. Stanford University Press, 1962.

ACKNOWLEDGMENTS

The index for this book was prepared by Mel Ingber. The editors of this book also wish to express their gratitude to Major Eric Anderson and Captain Peter Heffler, Office of Information, Secretary of the Air Force, Washington, D.C.; Master Sergeant Roy V. Ashley, U.S. Marine Corps Historical Support Branch, Washington, D.C.; H. P. Bryson, Cobham, Surrey; T. C. Charman, Imperial War Museum, London; Kate Clark London; Charlotte Denis, Paris; Vickie Destefano, Carole Boutte and Marie Yates, Department of the Army Audio-Visual Agency, Still Photo Library, Arlington, Virginia; Virginia Fincik and Dana Bell, United States Air Force Depository Services Section, 1361st Audio-Visual Squadron, Arlington, Virginia; Rowland P. Gill, Curator, U.S. Marine Corps Museums Branch, Washington, D.C.; Charles Haberlein and Agnes Hoover, Photographic Section, Naval Historical Center, Washington, D.C.; Geraldine K. Judkins, Operational Archives Branch of the Naval Historical Center, Washington Navy Yard, Washington, D.C.; Junji Kitadai, Tokyo Broadcasting System, New York City; Brigadier General Richard A. Knobloch (USA Ret.), United Technologies Corporation of New York City; Noboru Kojima, Tokyo; William H. Leary, Thomas Oglesby, James Trimble and Paul White, National Archives and Records Service, Audio-Visual Division, Washington, D.C.; Beatrix Macnaghten, London; Colonel Jean Martel, Musée de l'Armée, Paris; Carl Mydans, Larchmont, New York; Lieut. General Masatake Okumiya (Ret.), PHP Institute, Tokyo; Colonel Jean Parisot, Director, S.M.I.D.O.M., Versailles; D. Simpson, Royal Commonwealth Society, London; Richard W. Stephenson, Library of Congress, Geography and Map Division, Alexandria, Virginia; John Taylor and Sylvan Dubow, National Archives, Washington, D.C.; Thomas S. Terrill, Carlsbad, California; Douglas Thurman, National Archives Office of Presidential Libraries, Washington, D.C.

PICTURE CREDITS
Credits from left to right are separated by semicolons, from top to bottom by dashes.

INDEX

Numerals in italics indicate an illustration of the subject mentioned.

Printed in U.S.A.